The Wild Alliance
Awakening Your Inner Angel & Sidhe

Also by Søren Hauge
(In Danish)

Rosenkreuzerne (The Rosicrucians), Sankt Ansgars Publishers 1990

Det skjulte Menneske (Hidden Man), Borgen Publishers 1996

Selvopdagelsens Kunst (The Art of Self-Discovery), Borgen Publishers 1999

Landskabstempler (Landscape Temples), Visdom Publishers 2000

Daggry for Verden (Planetary Dawn), Levende Visdom Publishing 2004

Teosofiens Verden (The World of Theosophy), Levende Visdom Publishing 2006

Levende Visdom – Esoterisk Spiritualitet (Living Wisdom – Esoteric Spirituality), Lemuel Books 2008

Barack Obama (with Asger Lorentsen) (Barack Obama – Hope, Vision & Impulse), Lemuel Books 2009

Shakespeare Mysteriet (The Shakespeare Mystery), Lemuel Books 2010

Dine Syv Holotyper (with Kenneth Sørensen), Kentaur Publishers 2010 (Your Seven Holotypes)

Ildens Rejse (Journey of Fire), WiseHeart Publishing 2012

Englen i Dig (The Angel in You), Lemuel Books 2012

SIDHE - Elverkraften (Sidhe – The Elvenforce), Lemuel Books 2014

Vild Spiritualitet (Wild Spirituality), WiseHeart Publishing 2014

The Wild ALLIANCE

Awakening Your Inner Angel & Sidhe

Søren Hauge

The Wild Alliance
Awakening Your Inner Angel & Sidhe

Cover Design by Jakob Hauge
Book Design and Cover Art by Jeremy Berg
Edited by Aidan Spangler

Published by Lorian Press
686 Island View Dr.
Camano Island, WA 98282

ISBN: 978-0-936878-74-4

Hauge, Søren
The Wild Alliance: Awakening Your Inner Angel & Sidhe/Søren Hauge

First Edition May 16, 2015

Library of Congress Control Number: 2015937832

Printed in the United States of America

0 9 8 7 6 5 4 3 2 1

www.lorian.org

This book is dedicated to
The fellowship of Angels, Sidhe and Humans
In a new Alliance for Healing the Earth

Special appreciation to
David Spangler and all Lorians
For friendship and mutual inspiration

Warm thanks to Aidan Spangler
For refining my American English
And for proofreading

CONTENTS

The Wild Alliance

FOREWORD
By David Spangler

A new kind of human being is emerging, one who embodies a vision of the interconnectedness of all life and is capable of translating that vision into generative actions that foster wholeness and harmony in the world. Such a person demonstrates new ways of being on the earth, new ways of being human, new ways of being an individual. It's not that we need people of such character and vision in the world right now, though we most certainly do. It's not that such individuals might arise if we're lucky. It's that such people are emerging in response to the needs of our time, and they are bringing with them a fiery hope and practical insights to help others catch the vision and discover these generative and holistic capabilities within themselves.

Søren Hauge is such a person. This book is a testament to this fact and an example of the kind of service and wisdom he brings to the planetary task of birthing a new human way of being.

In the work that I do with Incarnational Spirituality, there is one word that describes the nature of the emerging human being. That word is partner. The world emerges from relationships of all kind, but among these, the ability to form partnerships, both for mutual benefit and for the emergence of new possibilities and capacities, is surely one of the most powerful and co-creative. But it becomes even more creative, more beneficial, and richer in potential when such partnerships are entered into with understanding, intentionality, and love.

This is what we can do. We can knowingly, mindfully, and willingly enter into partnership with the world and with all the life upon it. As we do so, there is no question a new world will emerge.

This kind of partnering goes beyond mere environmentalism. While it's good to be aware of the ecosystems in which we are embedded (and on which we depend for everything in our lives) and what we can do to help and conserve them, it's a larger step to see the world around us and everything in it as equivalent to persons, possessing their own will-to-be, their own paths of evolution and fulfillment, their own potentialities to discover and unfold. The new human that is emerging is not just a caretaker of the earth, a kind of planetary gardener and ecologist. He and she are participants in a community of life.

If this seems difficult to envision, much less to implement, it is only because we are so caught in old habits of thought and perception, habits that generally reduce the earth to a thing along with most everything else that shares the world with us. To paraphrase the theologian Martin Buber's important imagery, we live in a world of thous but we persist in seeing and treating it as a world of its.

It's in this area that we are fortunate to have allies, those who already see the world as a continuum of life and a celebration of possibility. Now, to facilitate the emergence of a new human way of being, these allies are drawing close and seeking to draw out our fullest identity as partners.

It's these allies, the angels and the Sidhe, that Søren writes about so eloquently and forcefully in this book, offering not only a vision of who and what they are but practical suggestions on how we can meet them in the proffered possibilities of partnership, finding in the process the angel and the Sidhe within our own nature.

These are beings of myth, folklore, and religious imagination. But they are also fellow citizens of the earth, fellow participants in all the processes that contribute to our planet's wholeness. They, too, inhabit a planetary ecology. It may be on a higher vibrational wavelength than the one we occupy and know so well as the physical plane, but the two interpenetrate and entwine as parts of the larger planetary whole. So they know what it means to live in an interconnected and interdependent universe. They know what it means to be partners. And with this knowledge, they know how to help us draw out the partnership identity that resides within us.

Like Søren, I have had the privilege and the delight of working with both Sidhe and angels. I can testify that within the "kingdoms" or wavelengths of life they represent, there is a desire, an intent, and a movement to come closer to humanity. They come not to fix us or to tell us what to do but to enable us to see fully and deeply who we are as beings filled with our own Light and sacredness; they come to help us see our own capacities as partners to life, partners to the earth.

The work of recognizing these capacities and drawing them out into expression is ours to do. They cannot do it for us, and frankly, given the single-minded materialism and anthropomorphism that dominates so much of human society, this work is definitely not an easy one. But it's the work of our generation and of those that follow us if we are to survive and thrive as human beings. It's the great task of our time and of the years to come, the task of discovering and expressing Homo Socius.

Though it is our task, we are blessed to have these subtle beings as allies. And at the same time, it's not a one-way street, for they have their tasks, too, not least of which is learning to see and understand the physical world as humans are uniquely equipped to do. They are, after all, non-physical beings (at least for the most part!) who are trying to come to grips with the challenges facing the physical world. For this, they need our help.

In the partnership between angel, Sidhe and human being, what is really being reflected is the innate wholeness of this beautiful and wondrous world. We have got ourselves in a position psychologically where we see only one half of this wholeness and for the most part deny the other half. This limits our actions on the one hand (and the fullness of our own well-being as well), but it does mean that when it comes to physical action and understanding, we are specialists! The angels and the Sidhe, on the other hand, see and know our world's wholeness and the depths of partnering on which it rests. What they lack are the particular insights and skills that we have gained through truly hard experience in what it means to be a self-aware, self-reflective, conscious being in the confines of physical matter. We know beginnings and endings, gain and loss, life and death in ways they do not, while they know the reality of joy, of life, of wholeness in ways most of us long for but never quite experience—or if we do, are unable to hang onto for very long.

It's these differences that give such potential power and promise to our partnership. They can awaken us to who we truly are as incarnate beings, to the wholeness of ourselves and of the world; we can give them an understanding of the divine mystery present in matter and of the skills of working with a world of defined limits and boundaries. Together, we make each other more whole, more skilled, more capable than any of us would be—or even can be—alone.

This is why this is such a valuable book, for what Søren offers us here is a description of this partnership and ways of growing into it together. It is a book for this time. May it serve the birth of a new humanity in which angels, Sidhe and human beings discover themselves in each other and rise from that discovery to bless the world and all the life within it.

David Spangler
Issaquah, Washington, USA, Spring 2015

INTRODUCTION
By Søren Hauge

Angels do exist. Real Angels. The Sidhe do exist. Real Sidhe. They were not invented for commercial purposes, or created in a religious context. They are living realities and they exist on many levels in a wide spectrum of variations. They belong to no religion and no culture. They have many names and they are described very differently in numerous traditions. They have been experienced and described by numerous observers that have encountered them and been communicating with them for ages.

Before we enter the arena of discovering and awakening our inner Angel and inner Sidhe, it is important to emphasize the living reality of Angels and Sidhe. They are living beings like you and me. They unfold, learn and mature in their own domains as we do. Some of the differences between us and them are mainly because we operate on slightly different wavelengths and densities. We are all fish ultimately swimming in the same Cosmic Ocean, but to some degree, we are separated in our respective locations, functions and abilities.

Let's start with Angels. In recent time, many excellent books have been written about Angels and I have treated the theme in several of my previous books. I warmly recommend prominent and globally recognized writers like Geoffrey Hodson, Dora van Gelder Kunz and Dorothy Maclean who have provided a treasury of insights about the Angelic or devic kingdom. Their testimony is a real storehouse of both common sense and intuition. We need a modern approach not weighed down with religious dogmas or cultural prejudices. Research into the Angelic realm is still a young discipline, but there is much to delve into already and Angels and the associated nature spirits are gradually becoming accepted realities as more and more people share experiences and let go of taboos from both the old, religious frameworks and the mechanical-materialistic paradigm.

My own approach has been greatly influenced by the insights from the theosophical teacher, author and clairvoyant pioneer, Geoffrey Hodson. This has been supplemented by the remarkable research into landscape Angels and the understanding of landscape temples, exemplified by the English spiritual teacher and clairvoyant pioneer, Peter Dawkins. During a period of ten years, I had the privilege to learn from him in courses, on landscape tours, during conversations and at events held in Northern Europe. To have received practical training, as well as spiritual teaching from him has been vital.

Some year's back I noticed during my morning meditations that a part of me was repeatedly drawn to southern England, and I was 'plugged in' to a specific landscape and its Angelic presence. I quickly discovered that the place was Sheepscombe Valley in Gloucestershire where Geoffrey Hodson started his deep cooperation with the Angelic world in august 1924, initiated by the contact he had with an Angel of teaching and wisdom, Bethelda. I swiftly set to visit the valley, and have returned to it several times. Most importantly, it opened for me an inspirational contact with the inner presence of the valley, greatly influencing my book, *Englen i dig* (*The Angel in You*). It also opened me to a very warm contact with the people living in Sheepscombe, making many wonderful things possible. It is a wise reminder of the principle that you should not just seek contact with inner guardians, but also cherish the outer guardians.

A short word about the words Angel and deva before we proceed. In this book, both words will be used. Speaking in general, they are two terms for beings in the same kingdom or domain. But in specific contexts there can be a distinction where *devas* (a sanscrit word from India) mostly refers to nature-related beings, while *Angels* (from the Greek word Angelos) tends more to denote beings expressing qualities not necessarily close to nature, and sometimes also used for beings more easily in contact with human beings. The distinctions can vary somewhat from author to author, and I have chosen to use them more in a blend in this work, at least in the first part.

The reality of the Sidhe is not as widely accepted as Angels or devas and their related nature spirits. Sometimes they are even confused with beings from the devic kingdom. Nevertheless, the Sidhe tradition is well established, and in the western hemisphere, it is particularly visible and accessible in

Celtic lore, mostly from Ireland and Scotland. To some degree, it is alive in the Nordic tradition in Iceland. However, as Ireland has the oldest and most detailed known lineage in the West, the Gaelic word *Sidhe* (pronounced *shee*) is used. In recent times the Irish seer, artist and cultural trailblazer, George William Russell (most commonly known as 'AE') has contributed significantly to documenting the reality of the Sidhe. His testimony as part of the Celtic revival in Ireland is remarkable. Since then pioneers like R. J. Stewart have played a prominent role, and teachers like Orion Foxwood, John Matthews, and recently David Spangler, have evolved the understanding of the Sidhe in different ways. In addition, artists like Brian Froud have opened new visual doors to the realm of the Sidhe – under the name Faeries.

Without my friendship and collaborative contact with David Spangler, I am not sure whether I would have opened my life to the Sidhe or not, at least not at this stage. He was exactly the right person in the right time and place, and he remains a wise teacher and friend that I am grateful to have met. His encounters with the Sidhe, and his ability to share them with others, are remarkable, full of profound insight, balance, depth and humor. We all need individual contacts and specific catalyzers to open doors in our life. Having been involved with The Lorian Association since 2007, I have enjoyed the mentorship, exchanges and friendship with a growing network of Lorian associates. The Lorian work as such is dear to my heart and an essential source of inspiration in my work as a teacher, counselor and author.

A few words about my contact. I call him *Fjeldur* although I should rather call him "mountain full of music". He is a Sidhe, closely connected to the Nordic area where I live, Denmark being the most southern – and almost flat – part of the Nordic countries of Norway, Sweden, Finland, Iceland, The Faeroe Islands, The Åland Islands and Greenland. In the Nordic traditions the Sidhe are called the Hulders (Danish: *Huldrer*), so I guess Fjeldur is a Hulder. The words mean *"hidden or secret people"*, and in a way, he is hidden from me, at least from my physical sight, but he is not a secret any longer or beyond my conscious reach. As a teacher in his own way, I guess he is a match for me. In the beginning, I received several visual impressions of him, but it is definitely his presence I sense. As a conscious inner contact, he is a clear individual with specific intentions and favorite interests. His collaboration with me today is, what I would call, a merging of minds. He eagerly suggests ideas and images to me, sometimes he unfolds a teaching as a sharing, and he always leaves it to me how to use it. I have also realized that he learns from me, so the relationship is a mutual sharing in confidence and with appreciation. His influence is behind this work. Fjeldur has supplemented and added to the perspectives David has given, and something new is emerging while still assuring continuity.

The background for this American book is the unofficial trilogy I wrote in Danish, *The Angel in You* (*Englen i dig*, 2012), *Sidhe – the Elvenforce* (*Sidhe – Elverkraften*, 2014) and *Wild Spirituality* (*Vild Spiritualitet*, 2014). This work is mostly a synthesis of essential parts of the three books, but it is presented in a new way with some additions, making it a complete work in itself. I am honored to be invited by the Lorian Press to create and publish it in US, and I am grateful to David Spangler, Jeremy Berg, Rue Hass and Lucinda Herring for their warm support and suggestions that helped create this work.

Søren Hauge, Højbjerg, Denmark, Spring 2015

I. WILD SYNTHESIS

Farewell to the Hobbit House

It is time for you to say goodbye to your habitual surroundings and begin the journey. Your daily life unfolds in comfortable and well-known surroundings where you follow rules and routines appropriate for your personal life. It is important that things function in a healthy, daily cycle so you can concentrate on your responsibilities and tasks and your relationships with family, friends, colleagues and networks.

However, when greater adventures await you have to prepare. This implies that you have to consider what you need, and what you have to leave behind you. This journey you will embark on does not have any outer equipment or preparations. In truth, you do not need anything besides yourself. Therefore you must be willing to do almost the opposite of what you know when you go on a trip to well-known destinations. On this journey, you need as little as possible in regards to cultural baggage, religious conceptions, national or ethnic habits, as well as patterns from your upbringing and education. In the widest possible way, you are asked to be as independent as possible and free from luggage, suitcases and trunks.

It is no easy thing to let go of most of what you have been raised to believe, trained to conceptualize and socialized to take for granted. It is very difficult. Again and again you may discover that you drag along with you heavy bags of all shapes and sizes. "That's how I'm used to doing it". "This is part of our tradition and heritage." "My parents taught me so." "This is the way we do it in my hood." "This is central to my values." On and on it goes. The question remains: How willing are you to let go? Do you think that minor adjustments will do for a great adventure? On the other hand, are you prepared for a completely different and much deeper process?

If you have to do something extraordinary, you must be willing to dig deeper, make yourself more inclusive and step out of your comfort zone. The Hobbit House is a warm cave full of lovely, recognizable stuff, merry tunes and cozy corners – all so intimately well known. Perhaps there is also occasional boredom there, but at least it is comfortable. So you think. Now the time has come to turn your head in a new direction and prepare for a real adventure that will be able to change things for good. Nobody can do it for you. You have to give yourself the green light. Are you ready?

The Wind Blows

"The wind blows wherever it pleases. You hear its sound, but you cannot tell where it comes from or where it is going. So it is with everyone born of the Spirit." (John 3: 8.) The winds of the spirit blow and they are free and not under any human control. Spirit, our deepest reality and inner being, is untamable. It cannot be subdued, bent or adapted to anything. It cannot be trained and made domestic and toothless. The conventional life we know so well is constructed in many ways upon compromises, adaptations and comfort securing survival, functionality, comfortable recognition and controlled growth. It is all reasonable and fair, seen from the mundane, ordinary life perspective. Nevertheless, the wild winds of the spirit often blow in the opposite direction of customs, habits, tradition, law and order. The security mechanisms, rules and regulations of civilization aim at securing and unfolding the well-known, daily rhythm with a certain calm and foreseeable functionality. Up against the daily waves of repetition, with only minor variations, the winds of spirit seek to stir, animate, vitalize and make possible new unfoldments and entirely new pathways. It easily provides occasions for collisions between daily common sense and the stormy renewals of the great forces. Conservative cautiousness collides with unfettered, propelling currents of pure spirit.

Spirit, the heart of sacredness, does not bother with strategy or political maneuvering, it does not compromise. It is unbound in its pure, raw nature. Love is not just being nice, just like kindness is so much more than the so-called civilized politeness. In a similar way, deep creativity is much more than, and very different from, the skillfulness of being handy. There is quite a distance between having clever wit and embodying compassionate wisdom just as there is a distinguished difference between moderate tolerance and deep acceptance. It is important that we fully recognize the rhythm of daily life and the practical values of numerable, splendid routines. However, behind, above, below and through this dimension something else is on the move. Into the stream of predictability moves something immense, which is high as a tower and deep as an abyss. This vast river of life is liberating, and paves the way to continents and sceneries never contacted or heard before by any human being.

Why Wild?

Why should we focus on something wild? Why should it be interesting to connect spirituality with wildness? Shouldn't spirituality be associated with education, culture and aesthetics? The question is fair. Are we confusing spirituality with something primitive and regressing back to vague shadows in a distant past when we insist on wildness? Objections seem reasonable. Spiritual impulses have refined human values, raised us above the so-called primitive and removed us from the savage and uncivilized jungle of survival.

Primitive means original or pristine and we can ask ourselves if we have lost some of our original insight and wisdom on our journey through the world of modern technology. If we mean depraved, coarse and blindly chaotic then it is not what we are dealing with. But it is entirely different if we mean something natural that has not been pacified and subdued by narrow norms and comfort seeking prejudices.

Spirituality in its most naked form is always wild and untouched in relation to the personal need for control, regulating habits and culturally accepted conceptions. The very idea that spirituality as such can be conditioned by public opinion, dominant trends and religious dogmas, is twisted. The fact is that the spirituality we witness in our human world and institutions is strongly reduced and limited, simply because many people have great difficulties in taking it in any larger dozes. Because of this, we have conditioned and bound spirituality in rules and regulations, theologies and dogmas, traditions and authorities. The pure face of spirituality has been too much for the human mind, which often needs strong boundaries, recognizable shapes and well-defined boxes. The way we generally treat anything alien, unknown and different displays the same tendency. In this respect, we seem to be at a very elementary stage, needing protection and guarding through rules and regulations. Wild Spirituality is what we meet when we let go of old moorings and dare to create new, unknown pathways and open ourselves to opportunities for bold innovations and synthesis.

Synthesis is dangerous for the unprepared mind that prefers to experience and divide everything into black and white. Synthesis is overwhelming and confusing for the calculating mind that always arrives too late at the train station of life. Synthesis is always wild as it surprises and amazes, wild because it renews and is dynamic, and wild because it cannot be controlled or pre-planned by the mind. We can calculate, deduct, add and combine – and no matter how many drops we count, they will never tell the tale of the mighty, immense sea. As long as we think in drops, we cannot perceive the ocean. In synthesis, we see the minute droplets, but we follow the flow of the water and the living, wet elements, waving, curving, streaming, surging and pulsating. Synthesis is the new emerging out of the known, with new abilities, new possibilities, and new qualities. Synthesis emerges when opposites meet and create a third factor with elements from both and yet more in itself. Synthesis occurs when sperm and ovum create the new embryo, when words converge into sentences and when canvas and colors join and become a painting. It is a completely new world, made possible by its components.

Spirituality in its most pure and undiluted form is always wild and untamed. *"The wind blows wherever it pleases"* and you cannot manipulate or dominate it. It has its own life, unbound and beyond restrictions. As soon as limitations are imposed the core drive moves elsewhere. Seen from here we can affirm that any interpretation is a limitation, and when denseness becomes too rigid, the animating, propelling drive is released and moves away. As long as spirit is fixed in forms, it will be adapted and colored. Some of the life energy remains, but the core drive moves in new directions. The more we are fixated on form, the more we limit and condition the very nerve of spirituality. The more we are open for the spiritual drive in and of itself, the more it can mold and define the expression, making it richer and more flexible, gifting the form with even more beauty and sophistication.

When we confine spirituality to rigid boxes, narrow conventions and rigorous cultural standards, it loses its momentum. It is a fact of evolution that this confinement happens as part of the process, but as long as it dominates, the conditions around spirituality will be poor. A message of love is diminished if it is restricted to love towards your own kin. Freedom is handicapped if it cannot manifest in society as a life freed from fear, prosecution and discrimination. Unique creativity is compromised if narrow prejudices strangle its activity. In addition, exactly because religious, cultural and ethnic norms are often massive and locked in, spiritual impulses will inevitably seem provocative and challenging. They will question the establishment and show new pathways that have not hitherto been tried out, discovered or even dreamt of.

Therefore, spirituality at its core is not just a comfortable extension of our usual life. Feel good spirituality is not necessarily the real deal. Trends and style can mask themselves as spirituality and of course it's part of the game of life that we learn to discriminate between outer appearance and inner mentality. Deep spirituality always challenges established norms and public opinion. Deep spirituality is always about liberation, freeing minds and hearts from the zombie-life that takes over when we accept just to be passive spectators and consumers blindly obeying the predominant zeitgeist. Even though deep spirituality is not plainly anarchistic, it has a revolutionary color. Jesus and Buddha were not strategic conventionalists or nice diplomats making convenient compromises. The crux is that you should not expect to arrive at new destinations if you insists on bringing your old house with you. You have to leave the known if you want to discover the new. Therefore real, living spirituality is wonderfully untamed, characterized by a liberating, surging flow.

Angels, Elves and Lovers

There is an important point throughout this book, that what we tend to project outside ourselves, lives within us and can be contacted and nurtured into a deeper, conscious unfoldment. As creation originates from the same cosmic source, the Nameless Sacred called God, Divinity, Brahman, Tao etc., we all ultimately share nature like fragments in a hologram displaying smaller pictures of wholeness within a grander scheme or greater picture. Following this, we can say that we contain within ourselves the seeds that have blossomed to the full in other beings that are not human. If this is a holistic principle to follow, we can talk about aspects of our nature that relate to the Angels, the Sidhe as well as to animals, flowers and so on. If we engage in a process that aims at cultivating our inner Angelic seed or our inner Sidhe seed, we activate this aspect and unfold it within our human nature. Within each and every one of us, we have domains and treasures waiting to be contacted and awakened. This goes for many aspects within our subconscious as well as our superconscious self. We are able to nurture these unrealized traits and hidden gems, bringing them to the surface by a conscious integration characterized by loving attention and deep understanding.

Two such major aspects are the focus of this book: Our Angelic or Devic nature, and our Elven or Sidhe nature, both intimately connected with our evolutionary journey as human beings. Both expressions of the Sacred have a complementary relation to being Human. Here we can also refer to a Human as a Lover, reminding ourselves that the unfoldment of Love has a very special role in our human lives. This sets the scene. As humans we have within us a strong – but for most parts deeply hidden – Angelic side, as well as an elven side. Both sides have been projected into religious dogmas and mythic lore, but they are real. Angels are real. Elves are real. Humans are real. We are siblings in the vast, cosmic family of evolving, cosmic beings. We are different, yet family. We are unique, yet united by major features that define our nature. We are creators, weavers and lovers together in unfoldment.

Within us, we have the keys to wholeness. We are fractals of unfolding connectedness. As human beings, we do not need to wish to become Angels or elves. We are already siblings and kindred spirits because we are in the same universal family. This is deeply meaningful, and when we take a closer look at our siblings or cosmic relatives, we can start learning from them. We can engage on an educational journey aiming at becoming more ourselves, becoming more mature human beings. This will begin to include and integrate more and more from our cosmic inheritance and in the deepest sense to become what we truly are. Considering how many problems we seem to have with respecting even our own, human fellow beings, this indeed looks like a gigantic task. The challenge, request and invitation to each and every one of us could therefore be:

You live on Earth as a human being, not as a transcendent, Angelic being or a mythical Sidhe. However, you can unite your humanity with the Angelic and Sidhe part within you in a rooted and yet heavenly way. This is your potential, no matter what kind of human being you are. How you do this is for you to discover as your journey of revelations opens to the adventure called reality. The Angel and Sidhe in you speak to your inner core about the most gentle and magical power you are destined to be. Unfold your wings and walk Mother Earth with tenderness and creativity so heaven can land in the world of manifested creation.

DEVA – ANGEL
ANGELIC ENERGY – CREATIVE JOY
"Attuned with living, cosmic laws,
Forms and expressions are created with ecstatic, light-filled joy."

Angelic nature has a multitude of facets, some of which stand forth with special clarity. Angels in their being are marked with a basic and unconditional joy, as shown in the motto above. This joy or elevated delight is generous and emanating. No energy is held back, nothing is reserved. This pure power radiates in a co-being, a sharing with wholeness. This delightful, sometimes even blissful joy reminds us of the basic innocence we associate with Angels – and children. However, this is not the result of childish naiveté, but a mature expression of their innate nature. Angels do not have our sense of heavy, condensed solidness. Neither do they experience shame, guilt or bad conscience. These are strange emotions to them and they do not really share or understand it as we do. Angels working in close collaboration with humans learn more about the human psyche, but still for them, it is like visiting a distant culture or country. The Angelic world – sometimes called the devic kingdom – is permeated by a permanent, vibrating joy.

Angels are focused on manifestation, on creating in attunement with the living laws of the universe. This manifesting process happens through their light filled being and is always characterized by inner and outer beauty, grace and elegance. In a way, we could say that Angels are natural artists. There is within their nature an effortless creativity, due to their inner unity with the greater whole and the descending tides that emanate everlastingly from higher regions down into the worlds of form. The Angels form patterns in light; they create the configurations and architecture of the universe – on all levels and in all sizes, from galaxies to subatomic particles. Because of this, they can also be called cosmic craftsmen following the living plan or the universal design molding the cosmos and its innumerable manifestations.

Because of the nature of their being and function, there is a simplicity to Angels' experience. They are not burdened by speculative doubts about existence and meaning, or purpose and essence. Everything they are in contact with is enriched by an inner livingness that produces vitality and abundance. They live in a state of freedom that stems from their inner concordance with the very essence of the flow of life. Therefore, they are always inviolable and rooted in centering in a way we humans often long for and hope to find. Although we can have this, we usually experience it as a lost innocence and something separate from mortal life. The Angels or devas remind us of the irreplaceable significance of creative joy and the importance of being attuned with the cosmos and everything around us. The devic kingdom is populated with countless myriads of our spiritual cousins from which we can learn. In this learning process, we can assimilate and integrate our own Angelic nature.

Connected with the devic kingdom and as part of this great evolutionary wave is a multitude of lesser beings, usually called nature spirits. From folklore, fairy tales, myths and legends they have a multitude of names. Behind all the curious conventions and stories there are real beings known by names such as undines, goblins, faeries, manikins, gnomes, sylphs, salamanders and so on. Sometimes the names and their associations can be partly misleading because they paint a picture with a blend of fantasy and facts. However, behind all this fantasy the vast world of nature spirits is part of the gigantic devic kingdom. Perhaps a very broad generalization could endow them with an instinctive consciousness while the Angels or devas work from a more intuitive awareness. While nature spirits tend more to be part of an instinctive, collective field, Angels tend to be more distinctly individualized.

SIDHE – ELVEN
ELVENFORCE – WEAVING WHOLENESS
"Within the weaving patterns of wholeness and earth,
Portals are opened to the light and beauty of the stars."

Like Angelic nature, the world of the Sidhe has a whole spectrum of qualities from which certain recognizable characteristics stand forth. If Angels are natural artists, we can say that the Sidhe are natural, weaving magicians. They can teach us how to reconnect with the lost magic of life. The Sidhe are our closest relatives and once in the ancient past there was no separation between us and them. We belong to the same life wave, but for millennia we have been evolving in different directions. If Angels are our cousins, Sidhe are our closest siblings, more or less disconnected from us for a long, long time. As the Sidhe have not descended vertically into our dense form of layered matter in the way we have, their course of evolution has been different and they have developed specific skills in their otherworld close to ours.

The Sidhe have learned to weave connections that facilitate and create wholeness. They are energy-weavers with an eye to all that connects and heals. Their specialized evolution has taught them to master the connective intermedium. They know the skills of being portals between divided realms. They stand easily at the balancing point between worlds and master 'between-ness'. Their Elvenforce also manifests in a sense for inner, organic connectedness, like living tissue in osmotic exchange and energetic distribution. In this living connection, the Sidhe vitalize and renew the energetic flow.

In their openness to the connective currents and all that renews and energizes organically, the Sidhe are also easily able to perceive the inner light potential in everything. This means that they are deeply disposed to quickening and bringing life to all they meet. As living portals, they can open themselves to influx from the stars and interstellar impacts and currents. They are conductors for energies that can imbue the condensed forms of life. They have a natural, imaginative awareness sensitive to light, an imagination of light that releases the rudimentary light within all life. In this is a redeeming magic because fixed energies can be released. When this is done in living movement, it is in harmony with the inner rhythm of the beings, things or situations involved. It is a spontaneous 'life-musicality' that becomes an organic mental and emotional dance. In the dance, there is light and beauty, releasing and bringing forth living wholeness. Here the Sidhe can unfold with morphing abilities. They are natural mimics and adapters within the flow of life. They can morph as needed in order to connect and combine, while they weave and dance and sing in the flow.

Connected with the Sidhe is a heterogeneous assembly of conscious beings, which have often been mixed and confused with the Sidhe themselves in different traditions. This is due to several factors that quickly becomes complicated to describe, partly because present knowledge about them is limited. Suffice it to say that these creatures are partly connected with the

Sidhe and to a certain degree they are offspring of some of the Sidhe emerging as hybrids. These beings are here called faeries (not fairies – the nature spirits) and are also known as fey. Sometimes faeries are connected with the Sidhe, and sometimes not. In their most pure expressions, they are deeply connected with the instinctive subconscious of Gaia or the Earth being we are all part of. In tradition and folklore, they are mythical creatures like satyrs, fauns, centaurs and other mixed beings. Geoffrey Hodson has described them as part of the domain of Pan. They are form-shifting mimics and intimately embedded within the dream world of the Earth.

HUMAN
LOVE – FIERY HEART
"Through battle, isolation, purpose and victory
Unfolds the compassionate heart, the fiery warmth of love."

As human beings, we are deeply colored by the fact that our line of development has brought us into a physical, compressed solidity. Here we sense the heaviness and density that calls for focused purpose and power in order to overcome inertia. We have struggled through many phases of evolution in this way and gradually we have learnt to master the ability to manifest physically – to form, manipulate and mold physical matter and to create our own worlds according to our wishes. Physically we are independently creative and perform with great individuality and with vast differences in all we process and form in our lives. We have also developed specific and distinct senses of purpose and the ability to follow long-term goals in spite of difficult challenges. This endurance in density and fighting spirit through all hardships is very human.

At the same time our descent into very solid and layered matter has had the consequence that we today experience ourselves and life as a reality full of separations. We often see ourselves as striding and fighting units in a hostile world, paving our way through the jungle of adversity and resistance. We have to struggle to maintain our own small island of security and the experience of being separate drives us to a gradually clearer definition of ourselves as an 'I', whereas the world around us becomes 'that' and people 'them' – away from us. When driven to the extreme we are alienated and everything outside us is potentially hostile. Our behavior leaves little space and consideration for others. This increases our suffering and we start longing for fellowship and belonging again. The long journey back from absolute 'I-ness' begins. Surrounded and permeated by conflicts we realize little by little that we need others and we are part of the greater whole. It is a slow and painful process because of our position in solid matter and often we forget to listen to other voices than our own inner choir of discord.

Our journey through the briar patch of challenges, dilemmas, opposition and antagonism leads to a multitude of battles, defeats and victories. The deep pain we hold and accumulate and the hurting we give each other lead to deprivation, regrets, humiliations and disappointments. Nevertheless, it also opens our eyes to the great significance of friendliness, generosity, reconciliation and forgiveness. Our hearts are tested in all possible ways, and slowly but surely, we learn the great lessons and gentle power of compassion and charity. Endurance matures in the beautiful blossoming of the heart.

Pain, loneliness and strife awakens the need for hope, and we light our candle in the darkness. We discover the irreplaceable power of humaneness and we realize that the fire of love is the greatest in life. The silent inner glow of goodness bursts into the steady flames of the heart that becomes the warm hearth of friendly gentleness and hospitality. Through the long, long epic journey, invaluable lessons and precious insights a sun of love expands in the human hearts. In this lies the great releasing power that redeems all that suffers.

As nature spirits are closely related – and part of – the devic kingdom, and as faeries are related to the Sidhe domain, so we can say that the incredible world of animals is connected to humanity in the physical, biological realm. Animals, including birds, fish, reptiles and insects, have developed many specialized talents, and many of these are very different from ours. Individuality is not the prevalent feature. The intelligence expresses itself as part of the species in a multitude of other ways.

We therefore have:

ANGEL ENERGY – HUMANENESS – ELVENFORCE

ANGELS
The Devic Kingdom with a specific connection to —> Nature Spirits

ELVENS
The Sidhe Kingdom with a specific connection to —> Faeries

HUMANS
The Human Kingdom with a specific connection to —> Animals

When we discover that the three waves can converge into a new river embraced and carried within our own humanity, we see a new possibility for living synthesis. We are humans and simultaneously we hold inner seeds and potentials that have flowered in the Devic and Sidhe kingdoms. We can integrate and add it to what we have already unfolded. The Angels and the Sidhe reminds us of vital aspects and skills we can embrace to become more universal humans, more Gaian humans that are able to take their rightful place within the greater scheme.

This is the Wild Alliance, the Wild Synthesis that we can start to awaken in our lives. For many of us it is a new journey. Considering that we have not even managed to create peace within all factions of our human kin, some would even call it premature haste. However, some of us see and feel the urgency and know that this Wild Alliance can help us become more embracing humans, so the adventure has begun. It will lead us into unknown places and areas, and nothing is given beforehand. We simply have to do it and we have already left the harbor. This is an invitation to you for a great adventure; full of risks and new challenges - but with great promises. It is a voyage of discovery into the land of tomorrow, starting in the here and the now, and we are not alone but assisted by our kindred spirits – the Angels and the Sidhe.

The Emerging Wild Alliance

What will we become as humans when the Angelic energy and the Elvenforce becomes a more integrated part of our lives? It still remains to be seen. If we perceive it as meaningful to integrate deeper levels of creative joy and magical wholeness, we must simply follow the flow and discover the fruits it will carry. While we cannot beforehand flesh out what it will become, we can certainly rest assured that it will help us become more whole and Gaian human beings. My Sidhe companion has suggested this picture as a possible help:

"If we imagine each human being as a loom with its numerous threads, the new synthesis or alliance with awakening the inner Angel and Sidhe could be pictured as new threads being interwoven in the web. The loom itself is the basic, human nature and the same goes for a great deal of the threads. The new threads have a different texture and new colors, which means that the pictures humans can weave and the patterns and structures created will have another effect – richer, with more depth and range. You are still humans. You are the loom. You have woven new patterns and designs into your collective palette." The same would be the case for a Sidhe. He concludes by saying: *"The Wild Synthesis is most of all a relaxed awareness within each other where we enter a shared space and merge with it until it becomes a richer version of ourselves. In the process, we continue to be who we are and blend with each other. The Wild Spirituality, the Wild Alliance, is the free spirituality where we give ourselves permission to weave new being, form new pictures and dance new dances".*

As a response to my description and illustrations of the relationship between the three waves – the Angelic, Sidhe and Human – he also suggested that I could use the tree as an archetypal and natural image for the new opportunity. The human kingdom can be seen as the roots, taking in energy from the ground and the solid, manifest reality. Humanity is the downward pointing anchor securing a solid base and giving the tree its juice or nectar from below. The Sidhe kingdom is the branches and the twigs reaching far out. The branches and twigs reach from deep below and high up making the tree an inclusive and manifold expression, organically distributing the vitality. The Angelic kingdom is the roof of the tree with the waving, green sea of leaves making photosynthesis possible, letting the solar light transform into life-giving power, chemical energy and organic connections.

This new synthesis will emerge in the central stem of the tree, the erect, standing power where the upward and downward flowing waves blend, letting something new emerge. The tree as a picture of the three waves and their mutual relationship brings beauty and wholeness into the center of it all. Each one of us is the tree. Instead of focusing on the parts, we can learn as stems to carry and be all of it. When we do that the tree will bear fruits and these fruits will be new in their nature – never seen before.

II. YOUR INNER ANGEL

Your Angelic Nature

You are a human being and now you live in a body in the physical world. In your inner nature, in your psyche, mind, consciousness and spirit you encounter qualities and forms of being you share with Angels. These core potentials and abilities are something you have in common with Angels and therefore we can say that they constitute seeds of your own Angelic nature. If, for a while, we can put our skepticism to the side and allow ourselves to sense and experience the greater being we embrace and are part of, a vast, deep space opens up to us, renewing and widening our sense of being in the world.

When we think of Angels with an open mind, we connect with a reality not contaminated and tainted with the cynicism and hardness that characterizes a significant part of our existence and identity. We can then feel and sense an opening into something real, uplifting and pure. We truly contact something that we more or less forgot when we as children started to adapt to the adult world with its harsh realities. In a way, it is as if we are receiving a gentle massage, helping us to let go of tensions in cramped muscles. We sense a numb, rigid condition passing and a relieving sensitivity returning, making us warmhearted and caring in a new way. We rediscover our humanity with inclusiveness and a larger capacity to expand and simply be.

Angels are often associated with being childish, and there are reasons for this, exactly because contact with them is a contact with gentle innocence and openness as light as a feather. We do not need to repeat childhood or to regress in any way. When we are adults, we are supposed to continue growing from there. However, we can rediscover Paradise Lost, the forgotten land of childhood, and regenerate our being in an entirely new way. This implies courage and a certain amount of wisdom in itself, as we need to let go of the cynicism and intellectual slyness that often takes center stage in the rough jungle of survival. We weave and include the most beautiful and delicate qualities in our adult robustness and little by little something new begins to dawn. We are given the opportunity for a new humaneness and something we can bestow on the world more valuable than the greatest profits and most impressive performances the clever intellect could ever achieve. This is not a small thing. It is this raw material the new world will be founded upon when we ultimately let go of the reign of greedy power and materialism.

As nature shows us the tender play of lights from the sun, flowing through the leaves of a huge tree, and the gracious melodies of birds in the summer breeze, so it also has the fiery power of thunder, the rampage of tsunamis and roaring earthquakes. This is not something that concerns good and evil. It is simply the multitude of voices in the mighty orchestra of Mother Nature. In the same way, we simplify too much when we only associate Angels with the light, tender and delicate. We are advised to be more inclusive, and not to be led only by our habitual coziness. Our inner Angelic nature includes the same wide spectrum, flashing and glittering from the wilderness of the spirit, and we can only let it live in our lives if we allow it in and learn to receive it. We can start to include new shades in our many-colored robe of multidimensional consciousness and by doing this we can also invite the Angels to show a new interest in the richness of human nature.

Your Angelic nature is close at hand, just like mine is. It is not distant and vague. It is only a question of giving space to it, and letting it color and affect all that we already encompass. Being Angelic is not becoming transparent and transcendent. It is a common misconception that we almost have to remove ourselves from this world, in order to become spiritual. Spirit has to be expressed more fully in matter. That's definitely part of the reason why the cosmos exist. Our mission is to weave strands from our Angelic side with all the good in our human nature. Then we emerge dynamic and mild, grounded and soft, anchored and expansive. Then we can take leadership and express empathy at the same time, bringing light, clarity, insight and creativity into our doings. This will make us into creators of beauty in the world as we keep our pose and dance with life. We will become focal points of being that invent, discover and apply new, useful knowledge in the world. With passion, we can become trailblazers for goodness, beauty and truth. In all this, we will be creative, soft whirlwinds in the great circle of life. Not just bleak, vague copies, trying to adapt. We will be poised, beautiful and attractive – both in our individuality and our togetherness and co-creation. All this will be permeated with the unique originality that arises from being in attunement with the presence of the here and now.

Let us therefore, you and I, embrace this journey and say yes to the awakening of our Angelic nature as human beings in the world. For the benefit of all. Not starting after endless deliberations, but beginning here and now.

I. Inviolability – standing in the living core

In the center of your being a wave flows, completely unbound by your genes, your environment, your culture and your nationality. It is a timeless, eternal being, completely beyond everything influencing your body and personal appearance. Its flow is finer than anything describable and stronger than even the hardest diamond. It is the very essence of your livingness, emanating from the immensity of spirit. It is a formless essence bursting forth, upholding everything you embody and express. It is a reality that is more than consciousness, more than energy, more than form – and at the same time expressing itself through all of your consciousness, all your energy, all your form.

You can call it whatever you want and it will just be inadequate words pointing at something beyond language. You can describe it endlessly and it will be like noise defining silence. If you have had even the tiniest contact with this inner reality and inhaled the scent of its flow, you will know – beyond any doubt – that your nature is inviolable and untouched by anything external. You will know that no matter what happens to you, the very core of what you are will remain untouched. This knowledge cannot be compared to even the most extensive and logical analysis you could come up with using the resources of your intellect. It is not a rational conclusion. It is not the result of accumulated experiences or learning. It is an instantaneous and irrefutable realization in your own being. It is a knowledge seated deep inside you, that you remain untouched in your core being. There is no reason for you to debate about it and you do not need to argue for it in order to keep believing in it. It is a fact in your consciousness.

In your inviolability, you have all the dignity that comes from a divine being. This is your royal nature, your majestic greatness, and it is completely natural and effortless. There is no need to cultivate an image. No self-evaluation is required. You rest unwavering on the throne of your living being. You are in the creative silence. You are composed. Around you, everything revolves and moves, but you are resting in your awareness.

When you are in touch with your inviolability – your unborn being – you are in the abundant flow coming from the core. You are in contact with the living force and in peace. It is not the peace that surfaces when unrest dissipates. It is a different peace, a reverberating peace. It is a peace emanating the sound of silence, a living peace that contains movement, and at the same time abides in serenity.

We often hear in the media about the importance of the sovereignty of a country, and that it must never be violated. A nation has the right to self-determination. It must not be compromised or forced by any other nation. You and I are nations in our own right. We are autonomous units and at the same time, we are responsible for caring for others. You are the authority and center in your universe. You are the reason why the billions of cells in your body cooperate every second, every hour, every day all of your life. You are the ruling sovereign in your cosmos, co-creating with all other sovereign powers around you. You are a star and together with countless of other stars you are part of a gigantic galaxy.

Think of a snow crystal. A complete geometry composed of a six-pointed star around a well-defined center. Unique, and yet created of exactly the same basic material as all other snow crystals on the globe. Same substance, same geometric frame, and yet unique. Two identical crystals have never been found. Think about the amount of snow crystals there are just within a square foot. Then expand to a landscape clad in snow. Then try in your imagination to proceed to encompass all snow on the globe. All snow crystals unique, no copies. Mind-blowing. In your inviolability, your deep-seated uniqueness, you are such a crystal, such a spark of divinity, together with all the other light-sparks in the cosmos – and all originating from the same source.

When you experience the daily challenges pressing you into a corner or into hectic activity where you lose balance, remember the center within you. Reestablish yourself as the guardian of peace. Take your place as the awakened being, always in the center. No power in the universe can move you from what you are. No situation or circumstance can force you out of your true nature. You stand in your inviolability. You have to be patient and practice many times. Quietly and like dripping water, accumulating and increasing its amount and weight, you will move your inner center of gravity. It will become more and more natural for you to establish yourself in you center and stand in sovereignty. When you rest in your natural dignity, you will feel and sense the living silence. You are permanently inviolable in your living flow, in your unborn, eternal nature. From this inner poise, three feathers or jewels develop – *Freedom, Livingness and Simplicity*.

First feather of Inviolability:
Freedom – unfolding your purpose

Freedom is a great and uplifting word to utter, but it is a far greater reality to experience when we sense and express it. When you stand in your sovereign inviolability, freedom is a fact. It is a freedom that is much more than just doing what you want. The inexperienced believe that everything revolves around the 'I'. When this is the case, it is important to say: *"I can do whatever I want"* and *"nobody shall limit my right to do this or that"*. This is not a great freedom. It is a very small freedom. It has its place, and it has its time. But one day you will mature, and see its limitation. Then you move your center of gravity and enter inviolability – your natural sovereignty – and discover an entirely new world.

To be bound or attached is to be imprisoned, to be a slave, to be dependent. The way to freedom is to unshackle, to let go of the chains that enslave us and makes life miserable and narrow. We are all involved in such a liberating process as we develop and mature, and when we discover all that binds us physically, emotionally and mentally. We are subject to an enormous amount of limitations and captivating programming. They come to us through norms, environment and public opinion. They are transferred via family, tradition and culture. They are transmitted daily through media and advertising. Many of them can be useful, but when they start to condition our very core and its ability to shine through our being, it becomes a wake-up call.

Earlier the world existed for you. Now you exist for the world. This is your new freedom. There is immensely more energy at hand, when the world does not just revolve around you. Great freedom is when you can offer your best and enter into creative availability in service to the greater whole. Earlier the world was valuable because you were precious. Now it is just as much the truth that you are valuable because the world is precious. The secret is that you are the world. Herein lies stupendous freedom. You are not just the limited part inside the surface of your skin. Your being is not skin-encapsulated at all. Earlier you were more narrow sighted in your perception and thought that your personal choices, values and behavior came first and the world existed for you. It was relatively true and had value as long as you believed it to be so. Now you seem to suffocate at the mere thought of just staying there. It was a phase. Now your center is much more integrated and your view is expanding to encompass larger and larger vistas. Today you see how indescribably beautiful and valuable the world is and how you can contribute to its growth.

Freedom in its outer form is the right to determine, believe, say or do anything. In its outer form, freedom is a right. In its inner meaning, it is something entirely different. It is a being, a presence. When this is consciously experienced, it is possible to be free even when you cannot assert that right. Freedom is connected with determination and decision and in its higher aspect it can be called purpose and essential nature, the ability to express what we really are. In our human nature we have followed our own will and we have developed a self-conscious awareness as a platform to stand upon. In many ways, through struggles and battles we have received what we wanted. We have also lost it again, and something new has been gained. We have become self-dependent. Now we reach for the Angelic part, which always follows the universal purpose, the driving force of wholeness. A greater fullness approaches. We do not want to just follow the separated self any longer. The new intention is to unfold our core purpose – to make the difference that arises from our connectedness with the greater whole. In this way, when we ask for universal purpose and the living laws of the energetic pattern of life, we weave our human striving into the web of Angelic purpose.

Freedom then becomes a colossal opening to vast space – inner and outer. Freedom becomes the liberating realization that you are connected and creative. In freedom you breathe light and joyful, and you perceive greatness. Freedom is width and breadth, the possibility to blossom exactly as you are in accordance with your essence. This is the covenant of universal presence. Energy circulates much more freely and you sense a greater pulse. You rejoice in sensing the wind blowing in the treetops and the joy of the skill in cooking a simple meal or greeting your neighbor. It is not what you do, but how you are present in the doing. Seated in your natural center you can be available and present. Not caught up in restless expectations or frustrating speculations. You are in your natural sovereignty. Therefore, the most natural response is to participate and connect, weave and manifest. You can soar as an eagle and walk in peace. Your Angelic wings can open for the becoming of every moment and you can be exactly where you are, letting the irresistible flow join your heart in action when needed and in resting when the tide turns. You radiate that which is real, the 'you' that is in the world.

Freedom is really your responsibility – your ability to respond. It is your responsibility to rest in freedom as you are, simply because you are freedom. When you are free, you are very responsible. You are no longer a slave. You unshackle and stand forth. When you are free within, you can respond in the outer, you can answer the call of life. In this way, you are deeply responsible – which means that you are deeply free. When you let your bird of freedom unfold its wings and soar, you emancipate a part of wholeness, bring it back to the greater reality and do great service to the world. In your humaneness, you join the Fellowship of Angelic Crafting.

Second feather of Inviolability:
Livingness – being in flow

When in contact with your inner inviolability, your congenital dignity and natural sovereignty, you can make room for the living flow from within. It has always been there but you have not been conscious of it nor able to feel its significance. This living current, this aliveness, will always seek to quicken and stimulate the situations you are in and open them to new possibilities. No matter how frozen things can seem, the energy will always seek a way to move. Do you believe this to be true? Do you have confidence in the ability of the natural energy to flow where the passage is, or do you prefer to believe you have to be in control, even if it results in collapse and ruin? It is a very vital question.

The flow of life is always heading somewhere, in new directions. Repetitions do not happen, but reoccurring themes reveal themselves in new ways. Life is always new. Routines and well-known tracks can create a basis, a floor – but it must never become a roof hiding away the sky. New life must flow as it will and if we want to control everything, it slips out of our hands and no surprises, no development, no new impulses occur. To say yes to life is to position yourself in the living stream where everything is in constant movement. If we are too attached to the past and to memories, it creates fear. We must dare to stand in the whirling currents where nothing is static or predictable. It is a mixture of knowing and not knowing, as when you watch drops of water running down a window. You have a clear sense of the direction, but you cannot foresee exactly which route it will take to come down. Therefore, it is an interplay between sequence and unexpected variation. Being in the flow implies that any mental operation is just part of something greater, not the factor that decides everything in itself. Neither is it entrapment within constantly repeated emotions, holding on to a too well known pattern. Deliberation and improvisation are like the two sides of the coin. Without mental structuring, there is a lack of nuance and ability to express, and without the spontaneous presence, there is no open navigation.

Livingness is the intimate awareness of inner currents and fluxes leading us towards melting, renewing and forming ideas, expressions and actions. In a river or brook, we can sometimes see fixed stones and the currents of water dancing around them. The interplay between the solid and the flowing is a good picture of the elegant relationship within us between the stable and centered on the one side, and the jumping and curving on the other side. To lose the sharpness and clarity means that we end up in the river with no ability to reach our goal. To insist on just looking firmly on the stones result in a narrow and limited view, and losing connection with the scenery. Balance is the key.

Another aspect of livingness is detachment from all sentimentality and no repetition of yesterday's agenda. The grip of the past is left behind and the new is welcomed. Do you have the courage to let go? Are you prepared to take bold steps into the unknown? Alternatively, are you encapsulated and merged with comfortable thought forms and well-established routines? If the first is the case, take a balanced and levelheaded look at the value of the past, and accept it as the conditioning that made the transformation of the now possible. Include and transcend. It takes adjustment and exercise to stand in the flow of livingness. Gradually you must get used to the new winds blowing from within, inviting you out on the adventure.

Sometimes it can be a good thing to remind yourself what can help you to stay in a fluid and nimble position in harmony with livingness. Be positive towards experimenting and exercising flexibility so you can discover the hidden resources right beside you. Remember to have a sense of humor and inner lightness, together with a friendly attitude towards people and situations. Above all, be as open and transparent as possible for each moment and for the loving guidance that seeks to help you every second in your daily life. Trust the flow as you trust how the ground carries you each time you take a step with your feet. Your Angelic nature is always united with the liberating, releasing movement towards greater horizons, new ideas, original solutions and a genuine, warm presence in the here and now. Life finds a way when we embrace that which is. Do not deny the voices that resist the now. Let them be heard as part of the present, and let them be teachers as well. However, do not step back from that which is, and let yourself be absorbed only by that part which was the past. Let the living wind refresh and renew you from within. Feel the movements of the breeze and befriend it. Respect its power and keep your balance, so you do not fall. Trust it as the perpetual song of life, telling stories of wonder and surprise. The wind is your friend.

Third feather of Inviolability:
Simplicity – abiding in greatness

Our life in the technological, media-dominated world can seem everlasting, fragmented and meaningless. What is up and what is down? What holds meaning and what is irrelevant? What is it all about? In a way, we can say that we have run wild in our gigantic, self-created maze of post-modernity. Part of the reason lies in the weight we give to the analytical mind and its ability to solve problems, create security and control its environment. It is incredible and impressive what we have accomplished with the practical abilities of the abstract and concrete mind. In the short run, it has left us spellbound and fixed on the power of the mind. We have created worlds within worlds and impressed our self with skills to such a degree that we have lost sense of the obvious. We have complicated ourselves into a brainy-smartness, running wild around itself and losing all sense of purpose and of the simple facts of life. Need has morphed into greed. Not because desire is bad. It is not. However, desire with no sense of deeper purpose is destructive and complicates because it rests on the assumption that the isolated individual is above everything else in a complicated world with no direction or meaning.

When you start being affected by the gentle touch from your inviolability, and feel the winds of freedom blowing from within, gradually the strange hypnosis dissipates. The spell dissolves. One by one, the complicated systems and programming's begin to fall apart and reveal their hollowness. Like in the film *The Matrix*, the intricate web of appearances dissolves into the basic units that created them – light and energy.

What is the deeper message behind the endless commercials and the shining facades, the promises and attractive presentations of the marketing world? There are no deeper messages. It is all about getting your attention and sell you something by telling a story you like. What is the deeper meaning behind the political spin and strategic maneuvers that create the daily headlines and the analyzing square dance of the pundits? It is all about clever manipulation in order to consolidate or change power. What is the reason behind why financial experts raise their brow or fingers evaluating Wall Street or The Nasdaq on television? It is simply that they discuss the movement of money, governed by emotions and gut feelings. There are no deeper mysteries here, except for the intrinsic logic of mazes.

There comes a time in your life where you start letting go of the numerous programs and systems. Not because they are necessarily dangerous or completely destructive in themselves, but because you have had enough and start seeing them as masks and security regulations in a mentality running in circles. You could not avoid the process or learning from it, and neither should you. In addition, you cannot avoid reactions from people still caught up by the game. However, for you, it has simply exhausted itself and you are entering a new reality full of new depth and meaning. Behind the facades, new life shines forth, gradually released by your awakening.

Life is incredibly wonderful and miraculous, not because it is complicated and more complex than the intellect can fathom, but because it is simple beyond imagination. Simplicity is the miracle. Moreover, the beauty of it all is that there is always simplicity in the complex. It is almost too good to be true, but the good news has longevity. Discovering simplicity is the cure we need to strengthen our awakening. The Angelic nature in us always perceive things from within, in their simplicity. Perceived from the essence, a given thing is overwhelming because it is so full of possibilities. The simple is not simply simple. It is rich and full in its dormant potential.

Living in simplicity gives energy to tackle and handle the complicated. You can live with it because you are not hypnotized any longer. You have a freedom and a vigor that makes all the difference. If your life lacks meaning and content it may seem to be a way out of it to dope yourself with endless television series, internet entertainment or virtual games. It is not a solution to anything and the frustrations keep piling up. However, if you have a rich life with real commitment, using your abilities to help and invite forth joy, then entertainment, internet and gadgets can be a brilliant spice, even a great teacher and help. The difference is huge. If all we take in is empty surrogates, there is no inner peace or happiness. On the other hand, if we thrive with joy and meaning, it can be good relaxation and less stressful learning as well, adding something to it all.

When simplicity is practiced, you experience greatness. It is not greatness in size. It is the greatness in the small flower, the blowing of the wind, the smell of fresh earth and the eyes of a human being. It is an unexploited freshness like in the early morning as the sun silently ascends on the horizon. It is rediscovering the miracle in the things close to you, the miraculous, sparkling newness you were part of as a child. Now you are an adult and you are overcoming the numbness of the post-modern zombie-land. You regain precious vulnerability and recover from the disease of cynicism.

Dating simplicity quickly becomes a deep love affair. Surrogates no longer seduce you and a stupendous world of real quality life dawns in your daily doings. You begin to discover what is actually needed here and now, and what you do not need to carry with you. As you do not chase the surface and its hollow effects you can save energy, reorganize your financial life and way of living. Simplicity has its own poetry. No one can tell you what is essential for you. Life is your teacher and the teaching lies right there in the daily affairs, not in longing for spectacular experiences and trying to follow complicated instructions from exclusive sources. It is a relief to discover that life as a teacher can take the most unexpected forms, and that you do not have to travel far to be on a great journey. Right before your eyes is the lesson of the now. Not in remote countries with secluded, secret masters. When you prepare to be receptive for what is right in front of you, and let it guide you, the next step is a reality. Around the corner, there is more to experience, but if you do not watch your steps right now, how shall you even reach the corner? It really is very simple. Usually your inner commentator is full of distracting bits and pieces from the past, or your stomach-antennas respond to repeated stories from long gone yesterdays. The often difficult, but very simple art is to arrive in the now. This is where it all happens.

A drop of water is a sublime example of simplicity. Its spherical form is so elegant and a masterpiece of complex mathematics. A drop on a leaf displays the same aesthetics with freshness and vitality. The elegant arc of its surface in its stature is a wordless poem of natural minimalism. The transparent delicacy can easily be scattered into countless droplets, and yet it stands forth as a majestic, sublime piece of art. You can let it fall on your tongue and it will dissolve. It is fragile and yet full of greatness. In our lives, we just need to become like drops of water entering the flow of the river of life.

II. Innocence – living in the pristine

Your Angelic nature is always a part of your natural innocence. This innocence seems to get lost for most people when they mature and merge with the adult world and its mixed, contradictory signals. Often we see the land of childhood as an idyllic paradise that has to be given up when we 'become realistic'. Part of that is true, except for the false assumption that the adult reality is more real than the world of the child. We all know this not to be true, but we tend to surrender completely to the conditions of adulthood. Why is it seen as a kind of natural law that innocence has to be left behind? This question is critical. We tend to succumb and give over childhood with no reservation to the harsh and cruel world of sheer financial logic and cunning. Why?

When we grow up, we develop self-consciousness, an important characteristic of being adult. We create an inner center, boundary or platform and learn to discriminate between I and you, between inner and outer, my world and the rest of the world. As a child, we had a symbiotic 'togetherness' with all around us. When raised and socialized, we became secluded as an independent force, and as adults we stood forth with a strong 'I'. Unfortunately, the contrast often developed to such a degree that we ended up as an abandoned island, lonely and full of suffering. We became hardened and the boundaries froze into walls in our 'skin-encapsulated ego', leaving innocence as a distant memory with cynicism and ambiguity as the rule. Luckily, the story does not end here. The very same innocence lost for you and I in the battles of life can be gently reconquered again with no regression into the past. We can be absolutely certain of this, because innocence has never left us. It has only been hidden behind the frozen layers of protective self-assertion that have consolidated for decades. The Angelic side of us knows this, in spite of all we are presented with from the world of sneaky commerce and strategic survival. Innocence is our natural being and we don't need to find it anywhere outside ourselves. It simply has to be uncovered. In your inviolability, you are always in innocence. However, you must consciously demonstrate the courage to let go of the artificial barricades. You must be willing to live in your adulthood with the vulnerability that is a crucial part of a more inclusive life. Moreover, that is not all. You must treasure the vulnerability, not as a weakness but as a clear strength, supported by your inner rootedness and living flow.

Your natural innocence grows in visibility when you consciously endeavor to be forthright and genuine, not only in your expression, but also in your openness with what comes from your heart. Innocence is the language of the heart. The strength of the heart lies in its complete transparency and this makes it possible to differentiate between mixed emotions and the clear overtones of clarity. The basic mindset of the heart – the heart mind – is openness and kindness, a hospitality free from calculating thoughts, burdening memories or limiting expectations. A pure heart is the nature of innocence. The absence of hidden agendas is liberating. There is nothing burdensome when the heart unfolds its nature. You can always sense the Angel within you through the innocence, gentle as a feather. There is a nimbleness untouched by the happenings of yesterday or worries about the future. It is a wholehearted and undivided presence here and now, right where life unfolds. It is a complete togetherness in this very now, light and simple. In this opening, things are magical because they reveal depth and possibilities. It is not a distant and fluffy thing. It is completely present and alive.

Innocence is unspoiled, untouched by norms, expectations, traditions and opinions. It is the real and genuine openness in the present moment and place, a passion to explore what appears, and a playful curiosity. Here you land in yourself without worries. Nothing has to be justified. You do not have to live up to anything. You do not have to attain anything. It is your birthright to let your heart sing.

It is a misunderstanding when innocence is seen as the opposite of wisdom and experience. Some of the most respected, wise leaders and trailblazers in the world show a wealth of maturity and competence while they dance with a smiling heart. They have stirred aspects of their graceful, Angelic nature and united it with their human authority and skills. Your invitation to dance with innocence is the most natural thing in the world. Why should it be an exception and not the rule? Follow your inner motivating drive for the obvious within your heart and you will become a guardian of tender growth, protecting natural living against the superficial clichés of cynicism and ruthlessness. By doing this you enroll in a new community and fellowship of millions of women and men all around the globe – all saying yes to the heart and the courage to be natural. This is not a small thing. It is in the forefront of innovative renewal. The reclaimed innocence is not a fashion trend. It is a heart-wave and its time has come.

Like inviolability, your innocence is your natural spirituality, the innermost retreat of your heart. It is destined to manifest all over and around you. Treasure and guard it so it can mature and shine forth. Give it space, so its three feathers or jewels, *Co-being, Generosity* and *Joy*, can develop.

First feather of Innocence:
Co-being – holding loving space

The rediscovered innocence awakens the Angelic nature within you and brings it into a new openness. The nature of innocence is not in any way fixed – it is an open space with its own inclusiveness. There is room to connect, room to sense the greater reality that is perpetually around you and within you. When you open to it and let go of the ingrained 'holding on' – you are invited into a greater presence that you have always been part of, but kept away from in your bolted reality-box where affirming yourself was everything and affirming life was nothing. Now you can partake in something spaciously delicate and immensely grander. The maturing that led you to be in touch with inviolability and innocence now gives you access to a greater world. In this greater realm, you are present all the time. You do not lose yourself, but you let go of yourself because you know that you cannot get lost.

It is like a bud that has grown and swelled in its solidity and influence. Now it gives itself to the light that warms it, and it can release and open its petals in complete trust and devotion. There is a new wide world outside the compact 'I-am-enough'. It is overwhelming and yet so very natural. It is life telling a new tale, a story about grand connectedness, where anything connects with everything. Nothing is separate. My 'I-being' and your 'I-being' have been given new layers of depth. We are together in 'Co-being'. We are particles in a sea of vibrating currents and we are the sea itself. This is not a theoretical concept. It is an inner experience of participation. Separation is a fact, but it is on the outside. The inner reality is unbroken and coherent. Everything is within everything else and in shared space.

You and I are cells in interplay, and together we sum up the greater organism within cosmic life. It easily sounds very pretentious when written or described, but experienced from within it is a simple fact – grand and yet unassuming. We know that atoms and subatomic particles are not at all like billiard balls or small, compact objects. They are, as we know it today, vibrating fields of possibilities, deeply connected and instantaneously affecting each other even across vast distances. You and I are also vibrating fields of possibilities, pulsating within the living, dynamic design of a larger reality. Instantaneously we affect each other, even in the smallest ways. Your mind and psyche emanates out into the greater sea of energy and you constantly receive impulses from the surrounding fields, especially those that are your closest relatives and contacts. It shivers, quivers and vibrates from you, and you sense how influences meet you from near and far. You are a living vibrator, a waving field with a temporary, dense form. This beautiful and intelligent form consists of billions of tiny wavy-fields, known as cells, and each of these is a world of untold numbers of atoms. You and I are therefore hosts for an immense universe of cooperative cells, all living in co-being.

Within this vast perspective, you can gradually discover that the heart is the center. It becomes your new GPS, showing pathways to the essentials in your life. When you consciously awaken to the heart in your center, it is as if space opens around you. Spaciousness and a mild fullness expands around you from within. You grow. The hardened, suffocating grip is loosened and there is space. The natural condition of the heart is to create space. This is the deeper meaning behind 'room in the heart' – to accommodate for heart-space, loving space. When there is room in the heart, a friendly and hospitable atmosphere arises and there is a place for recuperation, nurture and healing. It can only happen when you allow yourself to be yourself, free from burdening roles and masks.

This room of the heart holds everything and contains all that is good.

It is a gentle and peaceful place. You can experience it anytime and anywhere when you contact your center and become aware of the heart presence. It can take a little time, maybe because noise is roaming around in your mind and thoughts and emotions take all the attention. However, give yourself a little time and let it all settle, so you can discover the mild background and let it expand into your forefront. The heart has a quenching, calming influence on everything. A natural, living peace appears and in this peace, there is a smiling, soft warmth. It can also, at the same time, be experienced as a refreshing coolness, spreading out in your system. Just take time, listen and feel. It is measurable, even for scientific researchers who have now begun to investigate Heart Coherence and its effects on the mind, psyche and body. Your heart is a creator of harmony when you become aware of it and give place to its presence.

Your natural heart-space is a place where you can hold others. The most beautiful and simple way to care for others is to hold them in loving space. To give them a room that simply holds kindness. It is a restful being, not an active doing. You do not need to do more than create a sanctuary for those you hold in your loving space. Think of somebody. Sense them. See and experience them as they are in their natural, relaxed state, when they are at ease and in contact with their own heart-space. See them held in your loving sanctuary, included and surrounded by your wings of peace so they are guarded and protected. You are a safe haven, a refuge for those you hold in your loving space. Here you can honor them as they are. You do not need to do anything specific. You have provided the space for healing and recuperation, honoring and appreciating. In this sanctuary of peace let the silent, gentle magic work out in its own ways. You are simply there – no need to project, form or generate structures in the light – just hold the loving space and let the sacred be present for the ones you love.

What you do for others, you can certainly do for yourself and for all you contain. You can offer amnesty of the heart for all the refugees and outcasts within your own subconscious. Let yourself hold all the restless, wandering inner sub-personalities or inner parts or roles you tend to deny access or dismiss when they are identified – perhaps by other people. All your inner voices or gestalts that have survived in the suburban areas outside the metropolis of your conscious self. These peripheral voices or figures have survived, often in the shadows and outer regions while you were busy-busy and full of preconceptions and fixed standards. Now you can invite them to a hot meal and offer them light, warmth, friendship and a new life within your loving space. You can invite them back into your wholeness where they belong, and where they can grow, mature and transform. If you hold your loving space for those you love, in time you will discover that the same space gives room also to those you do not cherish in a personal way. At a deeper level, they are connected – and it is from this greater depth you open and hold your loving space.

If this is possible, you can also give amnesty of the heart to your own inner refugees, your beggars, robbers, anarchists, swindlers, vengeance seekers and unpleasant neighbors – the whole lot you have suppressed and denied because you did not dare to confront and own them. When you gradually invite them into the room of your warm hearth, without conditions and demands, but in appreciation of the light they have in their innermost, behind the distortions and high-pitched voices or low murmuring, animosity will change into new alliances and friendships. It may create tears and regrets over your earlier harshness and insensitivity, but it is only good. Now the time has come for reconciliation and healing. In the hospitable heart-space great things happen with the smallest issues. When you gradually learn to hold loving space and let your wings enfold the unwanted and rejected, it will transform as sure as day follows night. It may not happen within a blink of an eye, but you can rest assured that it will happen and that the small, silent and seemingly insignificant beginnings are often the most important.

As you grow in the ability to create loving space for others and for what you contain in yourself, it gradually dawns that something even greater, indescribable and fathomless is holding you. You realize that you are being held. At any time, in any place – you are in the palm of infinity, embraced by the profound mystery and generative source. You are being held precisely as the one you are. The holding power has no name. It is beyond all names and only becomes lesser by definition. However, it has been said that love is that which has no names. It holds you eternally in your being, as you learn to hold yourself and others. Invisible wings embrace you at any time, in any situation, and touch you with infinite gentleness. As you are held in this sacred space, so you grow to learn to be empathetic and embracing in your co-being.

Second feather of Innocence:
Generosity – radiating the essence

As you become acquainted with your innocence and your co-being, you discover your solar nature. The sun shines in the sky – that is its nature. The GPS of the heart always points towards that which radiates because it is the natural condition of the heart to radiate and shine. It is not an effort, a performance or a display of strength. It is your natural condition. Discovering this natural condition can be a long and gradual process, but every time you are connecting with even a fragment of this being, new doors open in you and you will never be exactly the same.

We often instinctively tend to believe that radiation is an effort requiring power, as if you have to press on turning the wheels in order to ride a bicycle or press hard and twist to open a can. Here we need another approach in order to arrive at the central point. The kind of radiation coming from the heart is not the result of a contraction of heart-muscles or another bodily effort. It is an effortless, unforced emanation descending from a greater being. It is an opening to the Angelic nature within you, to the natural light and kindness. It simply is and its very being emanates. When your inner sun becomes visible in the sky of your consciousness, you give your essence simply by being what you are. You do not need to live up to anything to be sufficiently good. There is a great and deep enjoyment in your natural emanation, simply because it embraces others and expands all by itself. So, to put it in another way: You give what you are. This means that you never run out of resources because you never end. There is no stock being emptied, but an opening growing wider and wider the more you make space for it. It requires exercising standing in your natural light, rather than reaching out for something outside yourself.

Think of situations or circumstances where you have witnessed somebody doing something exquisite for you or others. Perhaps you think about a crisis where financial help or practical assistance was provided. Was it really the actions themselves which made a deep impression upon you? Was it not the warmth, the genuine helpfulness and the light in the giving, that impressed you, rather than the physical changes themselves? An automatic supply has no depth. It is the human engagement that gives the magical ingredient. You know this already. An automatic raise of salary is nice and convenient, but it does not create deeper transformations. The magic comes from an entirely different dimension. It is the very quality emanating from another human being. The sincerity, kindness and generous mentality. That is the real X-factor.

When you do something for others, it is a transformative process when it stems from your natural generosity. Not because you are rewarded by being handed an amount of money or placing the other party in a kind of debt. In the natural state, you are rewarded simply by the sheer joy of doing it. The very action itself is a pleasure and generates a spontaneous joy and a gratitude in giving. You know that you make a difference in giving, and the value is shared by you and the others involved because you are connected in shared being. You literally do something good for yourself by doing something good for others. The secret in giving is that it is a receiving. It is a well-guarded secret, completely invisible for every egocentric person. It cannot be taught though outer stimulation. It has to be discovered from within, and when it happens, you are changed.

When you have started giving room enough to your heart-space and the sun of your inner being has started to radiate through the clouds of your evaluating and commenting mind, you will begin to experience the true joy in giving. It is a peaceful joy of radiation, marked by the sheer enjoyment of being part of wholeness and being given an opportunity to make a real difference. When you are lifted up, it is always good. However, when both you and others are elevated, it is simply wonderful. Real generosity is not something you show when you have energy enough to do it. It is something you radiate when you are simply yourself with no distortions. It is your nature and not something you transport or carry.

It is often said that we have to treasure "the small things in life", but what on earth is 'big' and what is 'small'? Misconceptions easily slip in when we talk about size. There are not just small and big things if we talk about daily life. It is more helpful if we say that there are inner and outer. Instead, we could say that we have to treasure "the inner things in life", which are always reflected in the outer. Real value comes from within. It should be an elementary fact, but it doesn't seem to be so for many people. When you and I realize this and act accordingly, it is a revolution. Nothing less. A genuine kind and helpful mindset can have much more far-reaching consequences than hundreds or even thousands of practical conveniences. Look at how gadgets like the cell phone or the computer have made the most incredible things possible – and yet, is it a guarantee of happiness? Countless people who were unhappy and distressed without a smart phone are now unhappy and distressed with brand new smart phones. Envy, bitterness, frustration, anger, fear and so on – they do not live in things, and they can never be ameliorated by comfort and luxury. We know that it's not wise to judge a book by its cover. We have to read it in order to value it. Life has to be read as well, and not just looked upon.

The Indian word for Angel is *deva*, and deva means *shining, bright, radiant*. When you start connecting with your solar nature, the deva within you is stimulated and starts to awaken. You will shine and radiate your brightness with effortless generosity. You don't expect reward or compliment. You abide in your being and rejoice in the light. This is the source of real radiation, deep charisma – soul appeal. There is no emotional strain and no trying. There are no declarations and assurances. There is effortlessness. Kindness is not a commodity. It is the flavor of the heart.

It seems strange that we can have such great difficulty in spotting something obvious. The truly giving nature does not announce its activity, just like you do not tell others that you will now move your legs when you start walking. When you learned to walk as a child, of course it was a huge thing. Perhaps you celebrated the triumph with screams of joy. They were happy, exciting moments, and very understandable. However, you did not continue shouting every time you took a step. You discovered that walking was natural and it became a means for something else. You could move your body and do things. It is the same with kind and loving acts. When you discover that you can create deep changes through your loving kindness, of course in the beginning it is fascinating. As time goes, it melts into your character and you no longer speculate about it. You do what creates change and it is very natural and obvious, and brings many good things to the surface.

In radiating your essence, you uplift and refine. It brings a unique inspiration that comes from you, as well as from the universal presence of life. The unique comes from your specific nature and the universal is part of the Angelic nature, pure and clear. The mixture of the two gives it a special beauty. You contribute by the very nature of yourself and by universal laws – and thereby you bring something new into being. The gift is your originality and your ability to transmit life-giving energy. The mixture of the original and the universal is very special and important. It can be illustrated by an image. No two gardens are identical but they all consist of soil, green plants, space and air. The specific arrangements and designs convey the intentions and creativity of the gardener, while the presence of the basic elements witness the presence of nature itself. The design is the human touch. The ingredients are the Angelic touch.

It is a gift to give, simply because there is freedom from calculation. You are not kind because it gives you a bonus. You are kind because it is a bonus in itself. It is a pleasure to give and you receive energy in the process because you are energized by radiating yourself. You partake in the great circle of life and give your contribution. The more you do this, the more easily it comes.

Practice makes perfect – as the saying goes – and the more you practice, the more it flows and moves. The sun is your natural being. No matter how cloudy it is in the sky of your consciousness, your sun perpetually shines. Shine on and let it shine.

Third feather of Innocence:
Joy – voicing the song of life

If the heart is your GPS, joy is the direction you take with it. You can be absolutely sure that joy will always be part of your natural being. If joy disappears from your life, it is a glaring reminder to you to rediscover your real track and renew your focus on your true path and destination. Joy is not a luxury you can hope for in a life supposed to be hard. Joy is an intrinsic part of your natural condition when you are open to innocence and your heart.

There is outer and inner joy. Outer joy depends upon factors you cannot always control. An act, an event, a lucky punch, a meeting, a gift. Inner joy is something arising from the depth of your being when you are plugged in to the greater reality. It does not depend on outer circumstances. If there is not an inner, conscious connection, it follows that it seems absurd that joy should be a source flowing from within. It contradicts established conventions and social standards. Yet, you and I are sources of a delicious nectar. This is an experience we will inevitably have when we open to the immensity within.

Joy is not a constant or unchangeable thing. It is a living wave with its own rhythms and facets. It can manifest as a deep, inner peace, silently expanding. This quiet peacefulness is like a quenching calm. At other times, it may be like a bouncy, dancing current, humming and chuckling with its own inner melody. In yet another dialect, it may be like a vast, warming river in constant abundance, flowing majestically and with grace. Joy is an ever-changing stream full of inner life, uplifting and with its own peculiar light and fragrance.

Like a metal detector revealing specific objects in the ground and like a radar able to detect flying objects in a dark space you can pick up the different tunes of joy with your being as you open to your inner landscapes and vistas teeming with treasures. Joy is not banal. It is not a tiny spice to make a bitter life palatable. Joy is in the very ground of your being and you start discovering it when you listen to the song of life, both in silence and in a multitude of sound filled activities. You can meet joy where you least expect it, but you can rest assured that can always be found where your deeper life purpose is and when you follow the visions of your heart. You don't have to earn it. You just have to believe in it and stay with it so it can flow through you.

Joy is always an upward moving flow or vertical movement, but it is not concerned with up or down as it is not the opposite of sorrow. It is an inner smile stretching over the horizon of consciousness no matter whether you are glad or sad. The joy arising from the innocent heart is not locked upon yesterdays or tomorrows. It is fully present in this now and not trapped in well-known mood swings. It is possible to sense it in the midst of difficulties and crises. It brings an inner lightness that lifts up, permeated with clarity and a pure frequency difficult to describe but very natural to experience.

Joy and amusement can be very different. While amusement can alleviate, deep joy is a healing condition. It not only relieves, it brings together separated energies and restores them. Therefore, joy is a great power, sought for although it is sometimes mistaken with cheer, entertainment and the laughter over being tickled. They can be related, but it is important to learn to discern and notice the nuances and differences.

Joy invites light into your life and loosens rigid thought patterns and psychic structures so energy is released. Joy is contagious and appealing like a medicine curing constipation of the mind and freeing heavy energies from closed circuits. It is like a playful wind removing dust with dancing ease. Joy is always an opening creating fresh air and room to breathe. Joy releases locked energy. Therefore, it is a very special, Angelic healer in your life and you should never ignore it.

It can never pay off to let down your inner joy. If you leave it behind you because of something else, you will experience a sterile and bleak condition in your life. You cannot live without water. You dry up and break into pieces if you do not let in the flowing element, fertilizing all the seeds of the good life. Joy is like water, sprouting and bringing life. When joy is watering the fields of your daily life, it calls forth smiles and humor. You can then be spontaneous and natural. You have faith in life and dare to look ahead. You know rejoicing is allowed, and that life is not just a mediocre affair, filled with the bittersweet poison of ambiguity. Doubt dissipates and gives place to a natural energy you had in abundance before you were programmed and socialized. You can be devoted to the present unfolding within and around you. Therefore, joy nurtures your optimism and makes you disposed to see possibilities and give the best a chance. Joy is the wings raising you up into the light where you belong and where your creativity flowers.

Joy has a sweetness that brings the best out of you. It helps you surrender to things you barely dreamt about and which you realize is your birthright. Joy is a timeless yet youthful energy we often associate with childhood, exactly because it is so often disregarded when we try to adapt ourselves to adulthood. It can be difficult to believe that it should have a chance when we enter the social and cultural stage with all its regulations, compromises and double standards. Exactly because of this, we need to reaffirm that it originates from the heartland of innocence, the very same world that we consciously reclaim. If we have the audacity, we will open the gates to true joy as the poetic, bubbling, intoxicating power that makes us wonderfully young and buoyant at any age. Joy emerges as the song of innocence reverberating from the well of life itself. It brings hope and renewal, and it is the serum curing the illnesses of sarcasm, callousness and toxic brutality polluting the world of so-called realism. The zeitgeist of today has been struck by this condition, attacking joy, sensitivity and innocence. Nonetheless, you can affirm your 'yes' to the inner flowering of joy and become a smiling warrior of peace. Let lose your inner Angel and give free access to the transformative power of joy as huge open wings preparing for flight.

III. Universality – engaging connectedness

When you look at yourself, it is often the easiest to start with obvious and simple facts. You are a person, an individual, with certain abilities, experiences and characteristics. However, you also have relations to others: family, friends and acquaintances. You belong to a family, a history and an environment. You are part of a culture and you live in a region in a country. This land is a unit in a part of the world, which again is part of the humanity to which you belong as a species on Earth. The Earth again is a planet within a larger system with the sun as its center, and the solar system is just a tiny flake in a gigantic galaxy, which again is just another microscopic fragment in a colossal cluster of galaxies within the vast universe. You are part of all this, even if your daily focus mostly is about such ordinary things as eating, sending text messages, following agendas and operating your lawn mower.

You are a human being with special abilities and gifts, qualities and interests. However, you are also the cosmic life expressing itself in a human form in time and space. You are stardust awakening to increasing conscious presence and right now have an organic form in the physical world. As such, you are not only an individual, a family member and a citizen in a country. You are a point of cosmic energy and consciousness. The universe has manifested at a certain point in time and space – as you. This is a gigantic perspective, but it is not more surreal than deadlines and TV-commercials. Your Angelic nature always perceives the universal perspective and everything that expresses universal laws and cosmic intelligence. No matter how much you invest your focus in the daily routines, there is always a higher and wider panorama in the greater space of your consciousness. Here abides your inviolability – and you are one with the flow of livingness.

Often we are so preoccupied with the daily tittle-tattle and routines that we blow small things out of proportions until they are hardly recognizable. If we hang on to these outer settings, we lose the very essence of what life is all about. It is healthy and appropriate that we raise our heads from the pavement and see the sky, the sun, moon or stars. You share destiny with the myriad of incredible life forms on Earth, from cells to whales. You share light, being and fellowship with all that lives. It may be that your daily routines seem most important while you are in them, but the things you cannot transcend, become your prison. If you cannot see where you are heading in a larger perspective, you never really arrive anywhere. You are just dabbling around, meandering aimlessly. This is not a petty detail. It has enormous significance. Your words and deeds affect the world in the most intrinsic ways. You are part of the greater, living, planetary nature, vibrating and affecting close and afar. Your choice of hair shampoo and potatoes, and your traveling destinations and choice of bank are all dynamic processes influencing the Earth and all its sentient beings. Your daily speech and the time you use in front of your computer are also energetic chain reactions, altering the course of the planet. You are a world citizen, a conscious entity in gradual unfoldment. All that you do and all you are vibrates and reverberates out into the grand physical, psychical and mental organism with pulsating echoes, infused with your qualities.

When you see at close hand how intimately you are interconnected with the rest of the world, it alters your approach to yourself and your own role within the greater scheme. You stop clinging to your 'skin-encapsulated ego' and with increasing hospitality you open the doors to the larger community you are part of while you retain your unique identity. You embrace your personal life and the larger life at the same time, avoiding suffocating in 'me-ness'. You bring your 'I' to the 'we-ness'. This is to develop the 'empersonality' – to use a phrase of David Spangler – the embodied, personified spirit, simply not taking things so personally but very authentic and present. In this way, you engage with your universal individuality and see the grand perspective in even the smallest details.

As you open to your universality, you invite greater forces into your living flow of being and awareness. You become conscious about your specific role in the Gaian whole of the planet and you can fulfill your destiny, your deeper purpose, if you follow your spiritual DNA with your core talents. From here, you can give your piece to the puzzle or greater mosaic and bring something entirely new into existence. You make room for your Angelic nature and affirm the commitment to create, form and develop in harmony with the cosmic pattern. In your unique way, you can express your spiritual intelligence in attunement with time and place. Maybe it is in cooking a meal, being kind and taking care in traffic, playing or composing a piece of music, making good teamwork possible or writing a column in the local newspaper or on a blog, decorating a table or building a shed. It is not about what you do, but how you express it. The universal touch will be either concrete or subtle – but it will be there.

Your universality is your natural presence, just like your inviolability and your innocence, the very ground of your being, destined to manifest within and around you. Treasure it so it emanates from you and transform into creative activity uplifting your world and the larger world. The three feathers of universality are *Light, Beauty* and *Manifestation*.

First feather of Universality:
Light – waking up to clarity

Awakening to your greater nature can be compared to moving out of a small, confined, dark room with poor air condition, and opening the doors to a huge world outside, with a blinding, overwhelming light and delightful air caressing the skin. The great world outside has always been there and nobody has kept the door closed in the narrow, shadowy room where you have been longer than you remember. You kept yourself locked in, until desperation grew to unbearable heights, culminating in action. Now you try to get used to the vast panoramas, the overwhelming light and delicate freshness full of fragrances, sounds and movements.

Your Angelic nature is always shining. It is not restricted to the usual black and white principles you know too well. As it belongs to your universal nature, it is full of light in itself. It does not need light from an exterior source, as its nature is luminescent and not bound to size, position or time. Its radiant luminescence comes from within. You have such a radiant light and perhaps it is the anxiety regarding its greatness that has kept you in darkness, shielded and seemingly secure. It was better to be limited and clearly defined than expansive and without solid edges. Perhaps that was your logic at the time. You needed a solid anchor, the sense of being you, and the freedom to consolidate. Therefore, it was all part of your unfoldment, your development. Silently you accumulated your experiences and then came the ripening and you began to experience the light in others, in the heart of all. It is time to step out into greater clarity. With a part of yourself, you may still believe it can be a threat to say yes to the light, as you might end up being consumed by it. However, with your greater knowing you are also aware that it is the habitual, self-limiting and protective voice speaking. You will not lose anything, as the essence that has ripened in the dark uterus is a seed of light and its nature is to be in its right element. Darkness has nurtured and supported the silent growth. In reality, this darkness is just the blackness of condensed light.

With this emerging insight, you leave the narrow backstreet of holding back and focus on your new adventure. As the caterpillar that has rested in the cocoon while it metamorphosed, you have prepared for the new phase in your dawning, epic journey – now as butterfly. You get accustomed to the bright world, and what it implies to perceive the grand perspective, where the small is big, and where what you thought was huge only turns out to be a minor detail. Things are turned upside down. A new order emerges when you take your universal position. Many things that looked deadly serious in your earlier life, now shrink to almost unreal shadows, or at least to minor details in the larger tapestry of life. Roles and masks do not bind your outer identity. You can approach them with humor and appreciate them in new ways. As you spread your wings, you reach for larger, far-reaching dimensions that include all your past and yet transcends it into the new and unborn.

Your inner light is your spiritual intelligence, your sense of what is behind the outer forms. You know that all things contain information. This information can be uncovered. The Angelic side of you knows that all things are filled with light and living knowledge. Nothing is separate. All is connected, and in this living web clarity and communication unfolds. When you plug in to this stream, you are instantly part of a quivering meshwork of living knowledge. You start perceiving the larger patterns knitting all things together. You perceive that all sentient beings can exchange ideas with each other. Information needs to circulate, combine and expand. With your new outlook, you see a city as a vibrating organism with countless multitudes of exchanging packets of light and information. The flow of cars, bicycles and busses bring people from destination to destination, moving energy and information. Goods are exchanged, conversations continue and deals are finalized. Electricity, water and heat make basic and vital functions possible, and in the air countless images, sounds and wavelengths buzz and move through computers, radios and televisions.

As you sense around you, so it is within you. Your cells and organs work nonstop to uphold, adapt and change the organism you live through. The synapses in your brain flash and pulsate in speedy exchanges. A buzzing, vibrating activity of information circulates and grows. The more you sense and experience that all is in perpetual interaction around you, the more you realize that the exchange itself is a constant sharing of light – of information. Nothing has value or reality entirely in itself as an isolated thing. It is in the exchange the flow is to be found. At a deeper level information is never a closed circuit – always a sharing and participation between elements or beings.

Light and information participate in this river of life and you are a point of living light in the currents of the flow. With this emerging clarity, this greater view, you can offer your knowledge and information in entirely new ways. Instead of only focusing on isolated data, you now appreciate the combining and uniting elements. You discover and perceive the greater pattern. Information and knowledge is only interesting because it is shared and circulated. Therefore, you must offer your light and clarity and make your originality available. You must have the audacity to share without being perfect. What can be finished and complete in the ever-changing stream of life? All is in the becoming - and so are you. Accordingly, you can only make the world a better place by offering your light and willingly exchanging with other lights. This is learning within the constant learning of the cosmos.

The more you see that light is knowledge and knowledge is exchange and participation, the more you can be free and unbound to create. You stand in your light and share it when the time and place is right. Perhaps you are most at home in the light of leadership and renewal. Perhaps you make your light best available in listening and holding others. On the other hand, perhaps you are skilled in generating the light of ideas, concepts and communication. Maybe you are trained in weaving the light of beauty or harmony. Alternatively, your light perhaps lies in detailed, discerning knowledge and specialized expertise. It might be that your light is a burning motivation in the light of devotion. Or your light is mostly characterized by creative rhythm and practical cooperation. There may be other forms and endless mixtures of light. Only you know and it is your task to bring it forth in your authentic way.

The nature of light is always transparent and sensitive to the greater pattern of life. Adjust your focus on this and you will be able to open yourself to a glistening, crystal clear awareness – like a window to larger wonders. The falcon eye in your greater being both sees the close and the distant, but never loses sight of the bigger perspective. Hold on to this and remain in touch with the greatness of life. This greatness is not quantitative. It is in the raindrop on the window and the wind in the trees. It is in the eyes of your neighbor and in a helping hand. When you discover the weaving of all things and the insights exchanging between them, the world is huge and awaits research, discoveries and revelations beyond imagining. Real knowledge is more in studying causes than just following the effects. Go to the source and understand the ripples and precipitations. In the human psychology the great causes are to be found in the core motivations and drives behind you and others. Research and investigate the inner reasons for thoughts, feelings, words and actions, and you will connect with the great currents of knowledge. See it, not only in personal interactions, but also in social relationships. Discover it in art and culture, in the media and collective decisions and get into touch with the driving forces. In the world of science, thinking and technology, you will see causes in the fundamental principles, ideas and laws. Approach the sources and you will much better be able to understand seemingly complicated signals, details and connections.

As you wake up to clarity, you realize the growing possibilities you have to create. You are here to sculpt and form light into new structures, new expressions and new processes. You are here to let the greater pattern of life radiate more fully. You are here to weave new connections, create new understanding, discover new pathways and see new horizons. Place yourself in your light and let it inspire you so you become exactly the creator you can best be – as a friend, a colleague, family member, citizen, human being and universal presence. Place yourself in your light and remain faithful to it so it can shine clearly in and around you and let your talents radiate for the benefit of all.

A crystal is a beautiful and accurate symbol for light and clarity. It is transparent and reflects light in well-defined structures and Angels, according to its geometrical form. It is loaded with information through its crystalline structure. In its pure form a crystal is almost condensed light, an icy structure of clarity and power. Mountain crystals and snowflakes are such expressions. Through them light glistens and gleams and matter itself is transparent. Let the clarity and precision of crystals inspire your awakening and stimulate illumination in your sharing and weaving in light and knowledge.

Second feather of Universality:
Beauty – breathing with grace

Opening to your universal nature and your inner light brings surprises. No matter how you are configured, little by little you will become more sensitive to the beauty of life. You will become more alive. Now and then it may seem as if you have never really been awake, or as if you are rediscovering something you left in your early youth. Your senses become sharper and vibrate in a more energetic way. Your eyes catch colors and nuances with new interest. Your ears listen in a more naked way to the myriad of sounds in your world. Smells and fragrances stimulate and awaken you. You taste things as if the world was new and your skin is sensitive to temperature and the touch of the wind and air. Even your breathing and your whole bodily sensitivity is awakened to new life. Adventure has entered your daily life and sleepy routines start fading. Perhaps only in glimpses to begin with, but gradually it will return more and more. Your wish must be a focused intention and not just a vague dream. Energy follows intention.

Beauty is a portal to the heart. It softens and increases sensitivity and creates room for gentleness and warmth. Its poetic nature is like a subtle, soft brook, increasing the influx of new perceptions and providing a deeper-rooted openness. You discover that all things have new aspects of refinement and power. Even the most banal cracks in a wall are a display of complex patterns like geological formations on Mars. You sense the unique in everything. The singing of the blackbird may be easily recognizable, but its melodies are never exactly the same when you listen carefully. Each and every tree grows in its own way and finds its way up into the light, unfolding its branches, twigs and leaves in a slow dance of universal laws and intelligent adaptation. Each and every cloud on the sky is completely unique and never repeated. The miracles of the world have no end when you start tracing them. The so-called trivial is rediscovered as marvels.

Perhaps it is habits, endless routines and programming into specific mental and emotional patterns that drains us of sensitivity and lyrical flowering. We are raised and socialized into letting recognition, comfort and control become the ruling factors in our life. It happens to such a degree that we end up deaf and blind to the basic unpredictability and complexity of life. The Angel within you is far away from the zombie-land of absence. It is in the burning now the portal to greatness is to be found, never in the shadows of 'not-really-here'. It is in surprises that we find gateways to renewal. Repetitions and memories are certainly important and necessary, but not as the alpha and omega of life. They create a sound basis, a platform from where we can reach up and out towards the unknown and the amazing surprises and fascinating newness that constitutes the core of evolution.

When the conveniences and comforts of our civilization sometimes fail, the typical reaction is irritation and nagging. However, it is a chance to rediscover the magic. When electricity temporarily fails in a neighborhood, people who have never talked with each other before start chatting and may end up helping each other. The GPS fails in a car and it becomes necessary to ask a local how to find way. Sometimes this can bring the most pleasant surprises. Inconvenience creates a window for unexpected meetings, and reflections on how easily we tend to isolate ourselves from others. In situations like these, when some things fall apart, there can be wonders hidden in other things, and the beauty of any situation may reveal itself. Beauty is so difficult to define because of its many facets, and yet we recognize universal patterns connected to it. Nature displays a mathematical, aesthetic poetry finding its way to the heart. The geometry of flowers is never boring exactly because no two flowers are identical. The green plants in all their variations, the playful elegance of cloud-formations in the world of aerodynamics and the sophisticated movements of insects; it all creates wonder and astonishment when we give it our full attention.

Even in destruction there is beauty, because the laws of nature are always at work and express a higher order of harmony. Chaos itself is well ordered. Because of this people can develop a fascination for destruction. The motive may be wrong but the aesthetics of a form disintegrating has its own universal beauty. The raging fire does not appear ugly as it consumes a house. The movement of water does not stop being graceful because it is the waves of a tsunami. With an opening to your light filled awareness, you can perceive great beauty in the midst of dramatic events and yet remain empathetic to human suffering. With your awakened Angelic nature, it becomes important for you to learn to express beauty in your own life. You need to bring living harmony into your daily activities so they can become a real expression of your inner grace. Independent of your gender, culture and abilities you must connect with elegance and balance. Grace is both masculine and feminine. Regardless of gender, it is your birthright to rediscover it in your mature adulthood and to give it your unique touch and specialized originality. Sometimes it is very clear how ageing brings its own beauty into people's life. That is why we talk about ageing with grace.

As you discover your new, growing identity as a universal entity, you start carrying your body with more dignity and refinement and new vitality is felt. You will seek balance so you shift between inner reflection and outer activity. You will seek and trace the rhythm of life that gives you better health and you will cherish light and colors that nurture the harmony in your mind. Your heart must be warm and your head must have clarity while you investigate and experience how your body is interweaved with your spirit. It may be inspiring to take a look at different spiritual traditions and see how they, each in their own way, have found simplicity and grace. The pathways are different and yet they are related on the journey to the same immensity, the source and mystery behind all manifestation.

The Zen Buddhist exploring the Japanese way of balance and the art of drinking tea. The Christian mystic that has found a way to grace in the gentle devotion to Jesus in the hearts of all. The Indian that has integrated the medicine wheel and the wisdom of the Great Spirit in deep and profound insights into nature. The Celtic Druid who has developed the skill of contacting the powers of the unfolding elements. The Daoist that has found the pathless path through water and fire, yin and yang. The Sufi dancing from the silent center or learning the mysteries of the heart through the practice of dhikr or remembrance. The ways are many and the richness in spiritual practices is great and full of variations. Nevertheless, in their core they are all utterly simple, leading to the breath of grace. You and I must find our way. For some the great traditions are essential. For others the deepest calling is not to follow a single tradition, or even to follow known traditions. No matter how your path is, it is imperative that you seek simplicity and follow the track that is yours. Insist on bringing beauty and living harmony into your life. Excess and going to extremes will temporarily lead you astray. Finding your way back to the elegant art of walking is crucial.

When beauty finds room in your life, the road opens for smiling ease, playfulness and the poetic mind, regardless of age and circumstances. The Angelic side of you opens to colors and tunes, forms and rhythms. You make space for sensing the shifting, rising, falling and bubbling nature of movements in the dance of life, but you also delve into the slow gradualness and the silent tranquility. You allow yourself to be spontaneous and to enjoy the delight of living now while resting in your inner center. You can encourage the beauty of structure and texture, of solidity and compact form as well. Beauty emerges in all of it. It is found in the purpose of all things, in their proportions and symmetry, their molding and stages expressing the intelligence of light. Density and lightness, moisture and dryness, movement and stillness – all are modalities of beauty. When your inner purpose and outer activity are in good contact with each other you become the artist bringing visions into reality. In this way you are a living piece of art yourself, a great work in progress. The more you insist on authenticity and on living your core values, the more your artwork will become an attractive, vibrant harmony allowing also the odd, quirky and so-called imperfect. You are part of this unfolding wholeness, and you manifest creative elegance in your own unique way as you find your preferred colors and tunes. Through you, the universe is manifested step-by-step in a way never tried and accomplished before, and through you the cosmic drama is enriched with new abilities and gifts.

Third feather of Universality:
Manifestation – expressing co-creation

As you plug in and connect with the deeper flow of life, you inevitably become creative. It is your nature to create something new, not just reproduce. The new is hidden as a possibility in your spiritual DNA and it is your life purpose to give it birth. As long as you just follow routines, norms and established conventions nothing significant will emerge from you. There will only be imitation and adaptation to given circumstances.

When you awake to your inviolability, your innocence and your universality, you are reborn in the world. This birth is your inner flowering, creating outer fruits. You discover that you are not here to copy or mimic others, but to bring renewal. It is a revolution in your life and it has massive repercussions in your relationship to work and spare time, to friends and interests, to family life and living. It is all influenced by the gentle shockwaves from your awakening heart. It will not take place unnoticed, and sometimes there will be thunder and rumbling in and around you.

When you manifest from your unique abilities and creativity it is important to listen to the rhythms of nature, in yourself and in the greater world surrounding you. Rhythms are phases or stages in the materializing pulse of life. Listen and learn from them and you will receive plenty of help towards your own accomplishments. If your timing is wrong, even the best resources can be wasted. In addition, if you miss the sense of the situation you will experience headwind when you could have been lifted up. The cyclic phases of nature are not difficult to spot. Actually, they are so simple that they are easily missed. The great circle is the yearly cycle, reflected in the lesser cycle of day and night. You know for certain that a broken rhythm can drain you completely of energy. In the greater cycle, the same applies. Wisdom can always be read in the great book of nature right in front of you. Your inner Angel is always attuned to the rhythms of nature, so when you start as a disciple or apprentice in the workshop of nature you exercise integrating your Angelic side with your humanity.

The yearly cycle is full of the most wonderful and surprising learning as well as ancient wisdom that never becomes obsolete. You can learn an incredible amount from this cycle of winter, spring, summer and autumn if you listen to its ebbs and flows in your creative life. It is always available and easily overlooked. Our technological civilization has taken us out of many circuits in nature and created a temporary numbness towards some of the most fundamental and natural things in the world. Many people don't even know how to walk in a relaxed way. It is as certain as day follows night, that nature is always our ultimate teacher. We do ourselves an immense favor if we apply the simple principles of nature in our daily routines. This will nurture our Angelic side with unimaginable ease. It is all about manifestation, about the flow of livingness following certain stages in nature. It is about accumulation and release, zenith and nadir, activity and rest.

Winter is the secluded, withdrawn phase where the vital energies sleep in the background and outer, reproductive activity in nature is reduced. Your inner being can open to light and heart space and you can be receptive for new, inner birthing processes. Spring sets the vital flows in movement and the forces seek upwards toward the sun, wind and freedom. It is the phase where energy turns extrovert and it is important to strengthen the determination to remain dedicated to, and centered in, core values. Summer is the culminating, extrovert phase resulting in blooming. Here the inner potentials from winter become visible and the treasures hidden in darkness shine forth. The energies of summer flourish with exuberance and color, munificence and sensible presence. Autumn is the concluding phase of creative culmination, bringing the lasting fruits of the yearly journey. The forces of nature show their full color spectrum and new seeds are sown for the next cycle. It all sounds almost too well known and simple. Therefore, the legitimate question could be why the majority of people do not practice it.

When you practice this wisdom in your own cycle, it is important to follow the sequence, be sensitive to timing and make it alive in your own processes. In the depth of your being, the chamber of your heart, you open to new impulses and follow the light of your heart. Then you affirm what you really need and follow the rising flow upwards, bringing things into the first stages of visibility. This will lead to the flowering of your inner endeavors and you start to see how much potential the initial impulse had. Finally, you will harvest the fruits of your cycle and discover the seeds for the next round. It is all very simple, very subtle, and requiring great human skills.

As your own nature is creative, the most important training must be in sensing and listening to what emerges from within. Be faithful to the inner motivations connected with your life purpose and specific talents. Everything else is secondary. In spite of the obvious, we know how easily we ignore the more important things. Our social conventions and traditions can easily lead us into ignoring our own perceptions. It is and will always be a core truth that if we remain true to our heart values and creative urges, abundance is at hand and we will receive help to succeed. However, we must be prepared to face opposition as a natural part of maturing, and we must be sensitive to corrections and adjustments in ourselves so we adapt and interpret the inner drive without distortions.

We are not only individuals. In our co-being, we interact with many others and as part of the learning process we receive vital instructions needed to make the creative work flourish. Creation is participation. It is never just an isolated, individual accomplishment. There is always co-creation at work. This means that you are dependent on others when you create. Even if you create beautiful pictures on a canvas in a remote place, far from other people, you depend on the work of others to have provided your working materials through their skills. You also depend on your surroundings, transportation, nature, weather and circumstances. You do not create out of the blue. You live and breathe in your creative flow with your surrounding world, which is your co-world. It is the interplay between your ability to stand in your center, and your relationship with the world, that manifests the renewal. It is futile to have good inspiration while being unable to connect with the world. There is a high probability that your drive will go down. Co-creation is teamwork, the ability to make your interior forces support each other while you reach out and connect well with exterior relations, friends and partners. Creative manifestation is the result of inner and outer energies playing together in the same direction. The secret in creation lies in the pulse uniting forces in concordance and making them play music. The saying then is that everything comes together and even difficult tasks seem effortless. This means that your thoughts, emotions and vital energies must cooperate and reach out in a concerted effort to your environment forging alliance-partners instead of opposing adversaries.

The Angelic nature in you is always in accordance with the laws of life and synchronized with the natural flow. It can be described in many ways, but an easy and clear approach to manifesting flow and creativity is the following anchoring points: *First of all* – keep focus. If you do not have a clear focus, which really is a purpose, intention or driving idea, the process will disintegrate. *Secondly* – be in the heart and stay heart-focused, all the way. Without heart-intention, you end up with something lacking soul. *Thirdly* – improvise after circumstances. You must intelligently observe the situation, adapt your heart-intention so it is realistic, and serve the real needs in concordance with the situation. Finally, *fourthly* – keep a sense of time and place so your creative intuition can be spot on with timing and a sense of situation. You need to know where and when to be with your creative heart-intention to let the magic of manifestation arise. Then you will sense the effortless intensity that characterizes deep, creative flow.

Everything in nature usually is in unforced becoming. Being a part of nature yourself, it is only to be expected that you can also be in this spontaneous movement. When energy is natural and surging, there is an experience of abundance, gratitude and joy. You will sense the living presence with your partners and in yourself, and there will be meaningfulness and a sense of timing. Natural flow is when the creative heart-intention is able to move from inner drive to outer manifestation. This is your destination. It occurs when your Angelic side arises within you and joins your human nature.

Pay attention to where you are, and which phase you are experiencing in your creative process: is it winter, spring, summer or autumn? When is it time to listen and attune? When is it right to act? Do you have good relations with your inner and outer partners? Are you able to hold focus and do you improvise and stay playful? Is your heart in it, and are you able to give it your undivided 'yes'? Do you embrace that you are here to create and that the greater wholeness needs you and your originality and authenticity? Questions like these are essential on the path of manifestation.

Angelically humane

No matter who you are, you are always a child of the wind giving you fresh air and blowing through your hair. You are a child of the sun, shining in your life and giving you warmth and energy. You are a child of the water, sparkling and streaming, moistening your lips and quenching your thirst. You are a child of the earth, full of fragrance, fertility and upholding care. Behind it all you are a star child, expressing your transcendent, cosmic nature in manifested worlds with a chosen form, to help you awaken to your true nature as a creative being. This is your human nature, but within you is also the Angelic nature united with the elements and laws of nature. This is your calling, your origin and destination – to eat strawberries, walk the earth, bring renewal to your world and rejoice. It is your birthright to hum in the light and be still in the twilight, to play under the sky and race with the flying flower-seeds. All this is taken in and lived out while you are full grown with your recaptured innocence, your re-clamed inviolability which you never really lost, and with your full, intact universality.

You are a winged creature, and you walk on earth. Your wings are your heavenly nature and your feet affirm your fidelity towards all creation. You are a creator within the greater creation. It is your nature to bring forth the new that has never been before, taking development into new pathways. It is your inner core to help in fulfilling the living purpose behind everything. You are not on earth to be a transcendent Angel. You are here to be human, but you can unite the human and the Angelic in a grounded yet heavenly way. It is your possibility, no matter how you are in your human configuration. How you do, it is for you to discover as your adventure reveals the next steps ahead. None, except you, can discover this. Nobody else can give you the clues, solutions and answers. It all has to be tested in your forge with the hammer of intention and the anvil of the heart.

Those who are still under the spell of 'Scrooge-cynicism' will call it humbug and the worst nonsense not worth listening to, when the Angelic tale of humanity is told. While we give them the full freedom to say and mean what they find right at the moment, nevertheless our answer is that – if the tales of the innocent heart, the sacred inviolability and the divine universality are just gibberish and prattle – we gladly choose the colorful dream and light filled utopia instead of the zombie land of pale shadows. We do it because we have experienced the greater reality, not just heard it from others or read about it in sacred books. We have tasted the food and not just read the recipes.

The pains, sufferings, and slavery of the human life is the story of how inviolability was replaced with restless materialism, innocence was substituted with the burdens of shame and guilt, and universality was narrowed to the separated fixation on the single self. It was all part of the journey into dense matter and had to take place in some degree in order to mature the individualized self. It has been a long journey and now this 'I' can meet a 'you'. Time has come for the multitudes of 'I' to step into the greater 'we' maintaining individuality and enriching the whole. We can let go of the self-created slavery of one-dimensional narrowness and step into the multi-dimensional vastness while preserving the essence of our past as jewels of experienced wisdom. We can unite the unfolding Angelic seeds with the uniqueness of humanity and start living an incarnated spirituality that brings heaven to earth.

Yet, the tale does not end here. Another crucial and deeply fascinating part of the epic journey has not been told so far. Uniting our inner Angel with our humanity is happening while we gradually learn that other chapters are waiting to be discovered, right now. This is the tale of the Sidhe, accompanying the Angelic music with its own tunes and melodies. That is where we go now.

III. YOUR INNER SIDHE

The Sidhe in myth and tradition

The Sidhe tradition is universal and belongs to humanity, not a single people, culture or nation. It can be found in different forms around the globe, colored with local lore, characterized by the time during which it flourished, and with diverse social, religious, artistic and cultural emphasis. In the western world one of the most prominent and remarkable traditions is the Celtic one, with a specific relation to Ireland, Scotland – and to some degree Britain in general. We will use the Irish tradition and lineage to connect with the Sidhe. It is also from here the word *Sidhe* (pronounced *shee*) stems. However, it is important to remember that the reality behind the Sidhe is universal and not solely Irish, just as the existence of human beings – or *Homo sapiens* – is a global phenomenon, called *mensch* in German, *binadamu* in Swahili and *ihminen* in Finnish.

Woven in a partly veiled tapestry of myth, legend, lore and history is the pattern that tells the story of the real Sidhe. We must prepare to be in the twilight zone between fiction and reality and not be too literal, while generally being willing to trust the validity of the existing accounts. The mythical story combines and weaves symbolism, the joy of storytelling and inner reality, creating a deeply fascinating legendary truth. According to ancient Irish history, the Sidhe were a people that came to Ireland as a tribe long ago. This tribe was called the *Tuatha de Danann*, the people of the Goddess Dana – also known as Brigid. Legend tells that King Nuada of the Tuatha de Danann wanted half of Ireland, but the Fir Bolg, the rulers of Ireland, refused. A great battle followed, lasting for four days, and the Tuatha de Danann defeated the Fir Bolg and became the rulers of Ireland. This was the beginning of the rule of the Tuatha de Danann, perceived to be a semi-divine race. According to tradition, the people came from a place West of Ireland, and in legend, this land had four cities, Falias, Gorias, Finias and Murias. They also brought with them four treasures or Hallows, a stone, a sword, a spear and a cauldron. They were supernaturally gifted, had magical abilities and were exceptionally skilled in arts and crafts. They ruled over Ireland until the Milesians from the South finally conquered them. Here the story turns in an unexpected direction. Instead of being banished, they agreed with the Milesians that they would keep the land above the ground while the Tuatha de Dananns were allotted the underground world of Ireland. In this way, Ireland continued to have two people – the Milesians above the ground, and the invisible people in the Underworld.

In this way, the ancient story tells that Tuatha de Danann became *Aos Sídhe*, also known as *aos sí, aes sidhe, daoine sidhe – síth* in Scottish – all meaning the People of the Mounds, as the sacred mounds – in Gaelic called *Sidhe* – were gateways to their domain. The proud people with the magical traditions were later known as the mythical Elves or Faery People – not to be confused with the nature spirits in the Devic kingdom. The Sidhe remained a people in full human size, living in a kind of parallel world beside the physical beings, but able to appear and contact humans if needed. The Sidhe, regarded as immortals, could walk among humans, and they became mythical beings endowed with eternal youth and beauty. Since then the Sidhe have been surrounded with a mixture of awe, fear, admiration and deep respect. They have been given offerings to ensure their goodwill towards people and there are captivating tales about their magical skills as well as scary stories about humans being threatened by them when they did not respect their rules and ways. During the Celtic solar festivals, they were remembered and it was common knowledge that the veils between their domain and ours became very thin. The Sidhe have been called *The Good People, The Good Neighbors, The Gentry's, The Fey, The Faery People, The People of Peace* or simply *The People*. Surrounded by veneration – and sometimes fear – they have been regarded as guardians of sacred places, mounds, stone circles and specific places in nature such as hills and mountains, lakes, forests trees etc. So-called fairy circles, also called elf rings or pixie rings, stem from this veneration. It has also been said that contact with this Gaelic or Celtic underworld was auspicious at dawn or dusk in the borderland between light and darkness.

In tradition and mythical lore, the Sidhe have been regarded as a kind of species in itself, closely related to human beings, yet in their parallel world able to do things humans cannot do. They can move fast through the air and they are form shifters. They have their special places of contact, like the so-called fairy paths that humans should respect. When appearing to humans they were often accompanied by vibrating sounds and energetic movements – sometimes called the *shee-gaoithe* – peculiar whirlwinds. Often, beautiful Sidhe-women appearing in green mantles with silver buttons and golden crowns have enchanted humans. The proud and noble Sidhe men often came riding on horses and there are innumerable stories about encounters with them. Traditions say that under specific circumstances the Sidhe could give humans healing, protection and teaching in some of their skills, for instance crafts and music. Humans were also able to visit them in the underworld, and if so, time would stand still and no aging occurred while being there. It has been said that poets and musicians were trained in their arts, and in Ireland the word *Ceol-Sidhe* denotes a specific form of Sidhe-inspired music. The beauty in this music has the power to reduce fear and make people fall asleep, or even to cure illness or heal wounds. The famous Irish harpist, Turloch O'Carolan (1670-1738), is one of the famous composers who heard and played Sidhe music. Several of his compositions are said be transmitted from the Sidhe to humans.

The so-called parallel world of the Sidhe goes by the Gaelic name *Tir na nÓg* (Tirnanog) meaning *the world of eternal youth*. This world is said to be full of beautiful palaces, treasures and haunting beauty. Life is in a state of youth and wonderful music. Leaves do not fall from the trees and you can smell flowers kilometers away. It is a kind of Shangri Lha and at the same time, it is intimately connected with nature. From ancient time, the Sidhe have developed traditions, crafts and skills in the magical arts. From their mystical origin West of Ireland, they brought the four Hallows, the Cauldron of Dagda, the Spear of Lugh, the Sword of Nuada and the Stone of Fal. When the separation from the human world happened, tradition says that the Sidhe took the treasures with them and accordingly the magic of the world was partly removed. However, that is not the whole story, because the Sidhe themselves were also separated, so their magic was impaired. This inflicted harm to humans and Sidhe, and both suffer from the loss.

The story behind the story

The lore about the Sidhe is rich and full of older and newer sources. People like Thomas the Rhymer (1220-1298) and Robert Kirk (1644-1692) gave valuable and deep insights. In recent times, W. Y. Evans-Wentz has highlighted the Sidhe in his comprehensive work, *The Fairy-Faith in Celtic Countries*. The poet and author Fiona MacLeod (1855-1905) was a pioneer in the reemerging understanding of the Sidhe and is well known to people working with the Sidhe. The spiritually oriented folklorist, Diarmuid MacManus, a personal friend of the Irish poet William Butler Yeats, gave new and living testimonies from Irish tradition in the work, *Irish Earth Folk*, first printed in 1959. One of the greatest contributors to insights about the Sidhe in the twentieth century is perhaps the Irish author, poet, painter, mystic and cultural pioneer, George William Russell (1867-1935), best known under his artistic and spiritual pseudonym, AE, who was also a close friend of Yeats. He can be considered a major bridge builder – bringing the mythical Sidhe into the real world of experience in modern times. For AE the Sidhe were not simply legendary semi-gods and mythical fantasy. He experienced them as living realities like humans, animals and flowers. He also experienced Angels clairvoyantly, but knew the difference between them and the Sidhe. In his pioneering, spiritual autobiography, *The Candle of Vision* (1918), as well as in many of his poems and paintings, he shared a wealth of insights concerning the Sidhe. It is an amazing treasure to be able to dive into his experiences.

This brings us into the present. Thanks to modern pioneers like R. J. Stewart, John Matthews, Orion Foxwood and David Spangler, it is possible to witness a new emerging view of the Sidhe, bringing us a new connection to our close relatives. This is a nuanced view equivalent to the modern understanding of the world of Angels and nature spirits. As mentioned in the introduction, especially the pioneering work of David Spangler is crucial to the making and outlook of this work. What follows as the background story is based upon the communications David has made with his Sidhe contacts and inner colleagues, and most clearly expressed in his momentous work, *Conversations with the Sidhe*, first printed in 2014.

This emerging perspective brings us back to ancient times, long before humanity began incarnating physically on Earth. We all have our origin and source in Spirit, the Generative Mystery. On our epic journey as evolving, conscious beings, we are gradually awakening to conscious participation in the universe. We are like acorns falling from the Oak tree to root in matter below, and to grow up as sprouting oaks in the becoming, finally emerging as tall trees. In the ancient past, preceding any publicly recognized records, humanity as spiritual beings started preparing for manifestation in the gradual descent into more and more dense matter. During the slow and long journey of denser and denser manifestation, very different experiences emerged for the multitudes of descending beings. These processes were prolonged and covered huge spans of time. Gradually very different interests developed. Simplified it can be said that many descending spirits invested all their energy in going more and more into dense matter. We can say that they chose the vertical descent. However, some of the spirits from the same life wave found it more and more interesting to investigate and experience in other directions. These increasingly chose a more horizontal descent and discovered completely different possibilities along these lines. In this way, 'The Verticals' went deep into layered, dense matter, while 'The Horizontals' explored the widespread areas in the regions where matter was not as strictly layered and densified as the regions occupied by 'The Verticals'. As this is a simplified image, we need to insert many angles between vertical and horizontal in order to fathom the complexity of the process. Therefore, there would be 'The Anglers' in many variations, adding many nuances to the situation.

The important thing to grasp is that this process and these different approaches and interests during the descent created a variety of developmental lines and a gradual splitting up between the multitudes of descending beings. As interests developed more and more differently, misunderstandings and even hostilities emerged between factions of descending beings. Step by step, a sense of 'us' and 'them' appeared and grew within the life wave constituting the archetypal origin for our present humanity on Earth. This was a process with many phases, and interactions went back and forth, but as descent and further involvement in different lines of development went on, separation and divisions became more and more strong. The different groupings of 'Verticals', 'Horizontals' and 'Anglers' diversified within their own ranks, and the result was two huge, divided rivers, each continuing on their varied courses. The 'Verticals' became the physically incarnated humanity, evolving in dense matter, beginning in the ancient past, sometimes known in esoteric lore as the Lemurian phase, followed by the Atlantian epoch and into recorded history. These diverse groups of evolving human souls is what we call humanity with all its lingual, ethnic and cultural differentiations.

The diverse 'Horizontals' and 'Anglers' constituted the other river, now separated from humanity. These evolving souls from the closely related, but separated flow, occupied regions less characterized by layered precipitation of denseness. This was and is the river of evolving souls we call the Sidhe. We can illustrate the different positions by an analogy from optics and the human vision. We use the term *central vision* to denote the part of the visual field where we gaze and focus. This is where objects and phenomena appear with distinct clarity. Humanity that chose the line of vertical decent into solid, layered matter, live and experience life as a relatively well defined world. The central field of layers in the mental, emotional and etheric-physical worlds are clear, divided and in increasing density as we know it. We live in the domain of divided particularity where matter is structured in ways we experience as relatively definable. This is our reality, especially as we have evolved into the present form of consciousness.

A wider field of vision, stretching out from both sides of the central vision, is called *peripheral vision*. This wide field is outside the area of the gaze, stretching from the very edges of vision, called *far peripheral*, to the somewhat more defined areas called *mid-peripheral* and *near-peripheral vision*, closest to the central vision. In this analogy, the wide world of peripheral vision is the world where the Sidhe and related beings live. Here matter is not strictly layered in well-defined levels of density. There are more mixed and flowing conditions. We are out in the twilight zone bordering day and night. There is energy and matter and the ability to form structures, mentally, emotionally and etheric-physically, but not in the same condensed, layered way. From this we can say that the layered-focused and the merged-fuzzy energetic totality constitute the wholeness of the created worlds, and we humans tend to see the first as the '3R', the 'real-relevant-reality', while we exclude and ignore the 'merged fuzziness' as the '3F', the 'fable-fantasy-fiction'. In addition, this to a degree is the story behind the division of 'The World' and 'The Underworld'. The Underworld is the world outside the human, central vision. It is the world beneath, besides and out of focus.

Here we have the background for understanding the two kingdoms, the human domain and the Sidhe domain, and their great differences as well as common origin. We are very closely related to our ancient Sidhe kin. It has been said that they are our cousins. Going a little further it could be said that while the Angels or Devas are our cousins, the Sidhe are our sisters and brothers of old. We have been separated for a very long time span, but we are siblings in the same ancient life wave. Suddenly we can also sense the cosmic story behind the legends of how the Tuatha de Danann fought against the Milesians and the war ended with a division into two, separate people – the visible Irish people, above the ground, and the mythical Irish people in the Underworld. It is also easy to understand why the Sidhe have been regarded with ambivalence – surrounded with respect and admiration on one side, and strict rules of 'allowed' and 'forbidden' on the other side because of fear when encountering them. Lastly, it gives us clues as to how we, when we again approach our Sidhe relatives – and they us – may rediscover the magical arts and begin healing the world and ourselves in new ways. Two complementary streams may merge in unprecedented ways. It is an epic story – perhaps especially because it is a story about ourselves – how we ended up dividing and separating, a phenomenon we know almost too well in our own human domain. It seems we are skilled in splitting and isolating and it could be time for acquiring new, needed skills of peacemaking and redemption.

Human evolution has been deeply characterized by obtaining abilities and qualities from experiences in dense incarnation and with a distinct differentiation between 'you' and 'I'. It has been very different from the much more loose and moveable experiences of the Sidhe. We may not really know all the intricate and sophisticated differences it makes, as we don't know it fully from within. Evolution in the mutable, peripheral areas of the mental, emotional and physical domains have given a fluctuating and vibrating nature that is much more fluid and energetically streaming than we humans experience. There has been a freedom of movement and a plasticity, we only sense in dreams and imagination. We are much more fixed in solid forms and it follows that our heavier and denser way of structuring and being active has anchored our consciousness much more to a slower, organic activity. Our physical experience is much more colored by separation and divided parts and objects, giving us a 'piece-by-piece' accumulation of knowledge and accomplishments. The Sidhe do not experience the same inertia and heaviness and they are much more attuned to wholeness. They are individuals like we, but more fluid and dynamic, whereas we are like islands of compact energy. The differences in specialization have resulted in two different species with obvious difficulties in recognizing each other.

We grow, mature and live as relatively stable and solid organisms. The Sidhe are capable of shifting their forms and appearance in ways we would call science fiction. They have their 'normal' appearance but are not locked in to the familiar grid of a constant look. They are able to form with their mind what they need in a given situation. Not unlimited, but with a flexibility that makes us marvel. They experience our static and stable forms as something distant and quite strange. Being capable of shapeshifting or morphing, they understand multidimensional energy in other ways than we do. As transforming agents, they easily adapt to situations and their minds are not structured to calculate control in a supposedly linear progression of events.

Incarnated in the layered and dense part of reality we tend to experience and sense the physical planet and nature mostly as a purely physical phenomenon. We have separated ourselves from nature by building our own worlds of urban structures and we consider nature to be made of useful raw materials and resources for our convenience. This is a partly sad but also understandable effect of our material, objectified identity. The Sidhe are far from this reality and in their different conditions, they experience much more the inner side of nature. In their domain, the mental, emotional and etheric-physical energies are intertwined or interwoven. Consequently, they are in intimate touch with the life side of things and sense the connectedness of all. They sense the streaming, pulsating dynamics of emotion and thought, together in the physical part of their so-called peripheral world we often term the Underworld. Subsequently they are in a much deeper harmony with Gaia or Mother Earth, our planetary being, and with the organic, inner life of nature.

For ages, the Sidhe have developed their civilization and cultures in the domains they inhabit. It has numerous expressions and is as varied as human civilization. At this stage we only have limited knowledge about it, mostly because they live in regions we will normally only experience with difficulty or not at all. This is mainly because we are not used to accustoming our own vibrational fields to their so-called peripheral regions. We are so trained and experienced in the strictly layered, central areas, that we easily omit and ignore the Underworld of the Sidhe. We have been told that they mainly differentiate between four regions. They inhabit what has been called *the sacred land*, corresponding to our plane of the soul and perhaps higher regions above the soul. Then there is a region where their *Sidhe civilization* in its numerous forms is mostly focused. Still, a third region is mainly built of *archetypal formations*, and it is from here we sometimes have impressions of temples and mythical places like the four Sidhe cities, Falias, Finias, Gorias and Murias, King Arthurs Logres, Avalon, Camelot and the Imladris or

Rivendell of Tolkien. Finally, a fourth region is described as a mainly *etheric nature region* of special places that most easily connect with our world, mainly through energized nature sanctuaries, ancient stone circles, mounds and magnetized power points in nature. We know something about selected places in the western hemisphere, but they also have expressions in all the other parts of the world.

The Sidhe themselves are male and female as we. Due to the condition of their fluid and mutable regions, they have a much longer lifespan than we, but they also grow and evolve at a slower pace, more organically and without the rush we often experience nowadays. They are not immortals, but because of their prolonged lives, mythical stories tend to portray them as semi-gods. They are our equals, but they have developed in other ways than we have. They have much closer, cooperative relationships with the Angels or Devas and nature spirits, and sometimes their appearances have been colored by this, explaining why there has often been confusion in this area, and they have been mistaken for Angels, and vice versa. As our new relations to the Sidhe develop, we will learn to differentiate more easily and get accustomed to our closest relatives within the planetary wholeness.

The new opportunity

Ultimately, the perspective behind the possible contact between humans and Sidhe is that it is all about becoming whole. As humans, we are in a complementary relationship with the Sidhe. They remind us of lost facets and abilities that we can re-encounter and integrate into ourselves. The Sidhe-Human meeting is therefore a chance to begin a deep healing process. To put it in simple and well-known terms, we can also call it a family reunion. This possible reunion or reconciliation will have far-reaching implications, and it will affect the planetary wholeness, the completeness of Gaia, the Living Earth with all its inhabitants.

As humans, we know about the pains of separation. In numerous ways, through wars, catastrophes, accidents and unforeseeable circumstances we have our share of experiencing how it is to be cut-off and separated from others. Sometimes it lasts a lifetime, and in other situations, we are separated for years or decades. It awakens strong emotional states and it can deeply affect our lives in traumatic ways, big and small. To be separate from relatives, friends and family can be very painful and it can arouse and motivate deep longings for reunion. This yearning is carried within the collective unconscious of humanity and one way it has surfaced is through religion. It is also a yearning that becomes very conscious when we experience how some humans act with brutality towards nature and animals. They are our co-beings and as species, they share a destiny with us on the same planet, Gaia – our shared home at this stage on our journey. At the same time, we do very hurtful things towards them. Our means of isolating ourselves from nature has also crippled us and made us weak in many ways as we entrench ourselves in our urbane reality. We see the yearning manifested in the current Green and Environmental movements around the globe, and the increasing struggle for animal welfare, climate protection, sustainability and green values. This is complemented by the struggle for human rights, democracy, ethical values and a fair world society with equal rights for all human beings, cultures and nations.

It is important that we do not get into unrealistic, romantic moods at this point when the hope for reconciliation with the Sidhe arises. As we know from our human reality, reunion can easily turn into new misunderstandings and hurting, if we do not approach it wisely and with an experienced understanding of the differences between us. We tend to hope and expect that others be exactly like us. This is not the case even between us humans, and it is certainly not the case when we deal with Angels and the Sidhe.

Our evolutionary tracks have been divided for so long, and our cultures and modes are difficult to compare in many ways. The gulf between us is much bigger than between the different ethnic groups of humans, and we have difficulties enough already. How shall we manage it? Will it succeed? What will it lead to? Many questions arise and we do not have the answers yet. There is a certain vulnerability when we approach ancient relatives without intimate knowledge about their customs and standards. To a certain degree, we are handicapped and both the Sidhe and we have our difficulties and challenges in this possible, new approach. We humans have numerous prejudices and many of us are buried in vulgar materialism and narrow-mindedness. Even life after death and immortality of all human beings is a long forgotten reality for many people. A willingness to let go of ethnic and religious biases is utterly impossible for perhaps even more people. So how on earth should we build bridges to a so-called alien race even more distant than people on the other side of the globe? Is the time ripe?

The answer is that if we should wait for the majority of people to accept renewal and bold steps before we went into action, we would be sitting inactive for a very long time. The majority of people have opposed some of the greatest artists, cultural pioneers, scientific innovators and spiritual teachers. Today most people do not find the music of Beethoven, the writings of Immanuel Kant, the scientific innovations of Newton or Einstein, or the civil rights activist Martin Luther King deeply provocative. Thanks to these trailblazers, millions of people can enjoy the fruits of their efforts. Today we are many people who can do our bits and pieces in advancing conscious awareness in many ways, and building bridges to Angels and the Sidhe, and nurturing our inner Angel and Sidhe, is certainly worth approaching.

We must not forget that the Sidhe also have their difficulties in a possible, evolving relationship with us. Our actions in the physical world, as well as our psychic and mental activities, have deep ramifications and affect them in their own realm. Our behavior affects them today more than ever and the disruptions we cause create reactions on their side. Especially our destructive conduct against nature and each other has consequences and reverberates into their world. Vast waves of pain, hatred, brutality, despair, sorrow, worry, fear and cynicism flood the borders and echo in their domain. They are not able to ignore our activities any longer and our noise makes them react. Warfare, hunger, inequality, ruthless exploitation and shortsighted solutions to challenges – it is all increasingly felt and the planetary crisis raises their attention in different ways. In the Sidhe kingdom, there is no agreement on how to respond. Some react by hiding away in the regions furthest from human activity. Their perception seems to be: How should anything good be expected from the primitive humans? What in the world could be gained in connecting with these blind and deaf creatures? Admittedly, reactions like these are not difficult to understand.

Yet, groups of Sidhe have decided to give their best to a new and dedicated approach. They have decided to make a renewed effort and see what fruits it will bring. They know it carries risks, but they do it, and there are indications that it is happening around the globe in different ways and in relation to certain people that are open and willing to cooperate and connect in new ways. The clarion call is motivated by the global crisis and the renewed effort to heal the planetary divisions and create a new course and new developments, free from shortsighted materialism and individualistic self-centeredness.

This is the common denominator. We inhabit the same planet and have the same Gaian home, even though we mainly live in different areas of the planetary household. The Earth needs healing and we all carry our part of the responsibility. The Sidhe have also created repercussions from the course they have taken. Like we they are in evolution and they are realizing their mistakes and limitations. The Sidhe also have their weaknesses and needs for new development. We humans must avoid catastrophe in destroying the Earth through our narrow-minded attitude, materialism and greed. We are so much out of touch with wholeness. Our human stupidity and heartlessness contrasts our wonderful potential. We have disconnected ourselves from the rhythm of planetary wholeness and we lack spirituality with its basic values for conduct and planning. Our behavior is one-sided and we seriously need a crisis to wake up to the required deeds.

The Sidhe on their hand are in danger of stagnating and they must avoid staying in their limited circuit, encapsulated in their remote regions, as in a pocket running out of oxygen. This is their dead end. In a way, they are in an isolated energetic bubble where they have explored and unfolded their own possibilities for ages and refined their abilities to create and build forms. They need to switch on their conduit to the greater planetary flow and become more connected with the layered worlds of density. Not all the Sidhe share this understanding, as some are still prone to choose the isolated course of survival they know so well. Deep down, beneath their reactions, the Sidhe share a sadness, well known in the Celtic tradition, and this melancholy also is a key to their longing for wholeness. Some of the Sidhe contacting us make it very clear that they really need to contact us in order to heal the ancient divides. They need to reconnect with the river of even greater wholeness than their own. They need 'fresh air' as we need 'inner life'.

There is no doubt that the new contacts between them and us are the beginning of a long journey, and there are many things ahead we do not know anything about. However, the Wise Ones of the Sidhe, the visionary pioneers from their realm, emanate an increasing eagerness. They invite us to a new adventure together with them in a new partnership. We from our side must carefully avoid idealizing them and trapping them in rigid thought forms, colored from the glamour we have developed about the past. It is very easy to keep focusing on them while thinking about them as magical semi-gods waving their wands, clothed in exotic mantles and with pointed ears as new age reproductions of the high elves of Tolkien. There is great inspiration to receive from science fiction, and the works of Tolkien are inspired and definitely have a wonderful touch of the Sidhe. Nevertheless, we must avoid glamorizing our partners and putting them on a pedestal from where they cannot cooperate with us as equals. Forms, phenomena and moods easily fascinate us. Due to our situation being in a dense, physical body, we have yearnings for beautiful, uplifting and promising experiences. That is one of the reasons why Angels have become so popular in our postmodern era. Some people almost worship Angels, ascended masters and radiant beings with a childish obedience as if it is a transcendent power not to question, but only to adore and obey. We are all beings in evolution and if we regress into an immature obedience and reverence, we deny our own dignity and we make real cooperation very difficult as it rests upon mutuality.

It can be very tempting to worship and obey the Sidhe, and as they are also very different and not all of them are free from glamour themselves. Being adored and the focus of flattery, sensation and praise is not a good starting place for a new cooperation. As they are skilled in camouflage and in mimicking, some of them might find it entertaining to 'dress up' as we long to see them, and play with us in a mischievous, curious atmosphere – not to do harm, but simply because they also are drawn into the glamour in their own way. We must do our best to avoid derailing our new connection. It is fully understandable that we find their nature attractive as they have developed skills and qualities we only have as seeds or almost forgotten potentials. We end up becoming bedazzled and blind of our own significance. Exactly because of this, we are encouraged to discover the Sidhe nature in ourselves and bring it into flowering. By cooperating with them and learning from them, as we can learn from Angels, we stimulate and nourish the aspects in ourselves and this opens the way for a healthy and balanced process, and we make it possible for them also to learn from us.

Right in front of us, we have a new possibility. If we use this opening wisely, it will bring us blessings beyond imagination. There are risks in any new adventure, but undiscovered worlds await us and when we embrace the new opportunity, we can associate with our Sidhe partners and let them help us awaken our inner Sidhe nature while we inspire them with our loving hearts, our grounded determination and our sense of purpose. We need each other. Hands reach across abysses. Bridges can be built, in spite of difficult odds. This is an invitation to a joint adventure, and for us it is this inner focus we are dedicated to nurturing. We will therefore embark on this epic voyage in order to engage deeply with wholeness and become Gaian humans. As Fjeldur has put it:

"The Elvenforce lives and breathes in the pulse that always moves and cannot be caught. The waving flow is as the winds that surge and dance, gather and release. All in nature breathes and in this breath is the Sidhe as ever becoming forms, expanding and dwindling in new expressions with elegance and subtleness,

rejoicing in the open flow and living in joy. The pain is also sensed as echoes from the valleys of fixed forms where distant relatives live, who do not listen to the call of the wind, the surging stream of the water, the scent of the exuberant earth and the song of the sparkling rays of the sun. This distant kin creates noise and battle in heavy denseness. Yet, it is a family member of the light and the call goes from the wide winds to all four corners of Gaia to distant regions: It is the time for new steps that even we – the living relatives of the wind and the growth – must abide. The Earth breathes and the erect nobleness is sensed with the waving, streaming presence. We – the Sidhe – come to you. Let us learn to be together. Let us be in fellowship. Let us discover the next steps together."

Tracing the Stone and the Dancer

We must find the deep calm of the standing stones, rooted below and reaching up into the open air. We must become the stone, standing in serenity. This is where the journey begins. When we find home so we can stand in ourselves, we become columns linking heaven and Earth. This is a silent process and it increases gradually and naturally. Before we become standing stones, we have not yet discovered our inherent power. It is a silent power, flowing from our inner source, with no sounds, colors or forms. Something in us must consolidate through the challenges and learnings of life. First, we mature into personal strength and breakthrough power. Later we walk over the ruins of our own narrow-mindedness and through inevitable crises; we start to open to the softness of the heart, making us inclusive in new ways. We let go of the bulwarks of the ego and our personal presence becomes gentler and with more relaxed dignity. Then comes the time where we can become standing stones of beauty and gentle power in our world.

When standing in your being, you can protect and build bridges simultaneously. The art of guarding borders is significant. When we can cherish our own inner world and uphold our boundaries, then we can also protect and honor the boundaries of others and support the valuable beings we meet on our way. It is all about honoring life, the life in you and in others.

When we can guard the thresholds, we can become bridge builders and initiate contact, movement and flow between separated worlds. We know about the challenges in this when we have to alleviate animosity between opposing parties, create understanding between cultures, ethnic groups, religions or even neighbors.

The Sidhe have been standing stones in their own way for ages. Not in the physical forms we are accustomed to, but as living portals in light. They have a certain lightness and yet they have worn the mantle of responsibility to guard thresholds between worlds. There is an art we can learn here, an entirely new learning so we can start healing the divisions between our cultural reality and the world of nature. There are many layers and aspects of this noble art. Stable bridges and well-functioning columns are needed when new portals have to be made. It is a surfing and weaving art, requiring a dancing mentality we can also learn from our Sidhe partners. It is an alchemical art to let these two opposites join hands. We may ask ourselves: What happens, when the associative and spontaneous meet the precise and focused? What is developed when we unite the lyrical and the logical? What is the result of letting objective units and subjective connection blend in joint process? What will it mean when we reunite nature with culture? These are only preliminary questions. They are just the beginning. Some may ask why we should need the Sidhe to nurture this aspect within ourselves, and the answer is that we would probably be able to do it on our own anyway, but the course would be much, much more slow and lingering. Why not accept a helping hand and let the presence of our ancient kinfolks hasten the process significantly and make it safer, while we at the same time start a new collaboration in service of all living beings on the planet?

We – you and me – are invited to a new dance, a new erectness in living peace. This is the ability to stand elegantly like a reed in the wind, uniting force and twirling, manifesting power and grace. When we do this, we become the living stones. This is the Elvenforce, full of undiscovered magic. It is within us, waiting to be stirred. It is our true fairy tale. The journey from the stone to the dancer is our legendary voyage of awakening our inner Sidhe. This noble art of *the Stone and the Dancer* can also be called *the tale of the Tree and the Wind,* or *the Harp and the Tunes.*

The journey leads through four portals, four directions, four worlds, together creating a complete circle. These four worlds and the portals leading to them open to domains within you that you may have forgotten or repressed, or you may simply feel that they are difficult to have in your ordinary life. They are doorways to the ancient and eternally young Sidhe-wisdom, going back to the dawn of time. They are also insights helping you today where you seek greater wholeness, and to rediscover magic and lost innocence. Now the time has come to open the wild portals and let them invite you in. If you follow trustfully, you will not remain the same. You do not need to understand in your usual ways. Just let it in and let it work. It is like a fairy tale, but it is very real as faeries are real. Come! Follow. Now it begins. We start in the North.

The Portal of the North

SILENTLY RESTS THE FORCE
SILENTLY RESTS THE FORCE
AT THE ROOT OF THE MOUNTAIN

SILENTLY SMILES THE FORCE
SILENTLY SMILES THE FORCE
AT THE FEET OF THE PILGRIM

FROM HERE THE JOURNEY BEGINS - TO DISTANT PLACES
WITH THE BACK FACING NORTH

ONLY THE HEART CAN BRING PEACE
AND EMBRACE
WHERE THE LIFE-FORCE ABIDES

Qualities: Rooting, Landing, Portal
Element: Earth
Treasure: Stone
Keyword: Force

There is a portal in the North you must reach on your journey. In order to reach your destination you must lean your back towards the North, as you have never done before. You must decide to find yourself with unwavering determination as you do when something is crucial. Look at your compass and let the pointer towards North show you the way. Ally yourself with silent strength, natural authority and steadfastness. Countless things may try to prevent you from arriving and they will all have plenty of clever reasons and specious alternatives for holding you back. *"Why waste your* *time going North? There are countless other things to do".* Your answer can only be that no matter how convincing it may sound, you simply have to follow your inner call to go North. It is as crucial as breathing, just as significant as standing up in the morning and facing the day. Therefore, you cannot be swayed, and you go North.

When you arrive, you have no doubt. You know, as certain as anything, that you are in the North and deep within, you always knew that North was there and in you there was a door leading to this magical place. In front of you are great, beautiful mountains, reaching majestically towards the night sky. Up there, the gleaming lights of the stars twinkle, and you sense how you are connected with the greatness and evocative vastness, calling you. The starlight in the dark night reminds you that you are a star being and it is your destiny to rediscover the magic that was lost when you were absorbed by the surrogate-world of hollow values. None other than yourself has drawn you from life, the great life. None other than you can bring you back.

As you behold the majestic presence of the mountains and the beauty of the starry heaven, you inhale the fragrance of fir trees and sense the forests surrounding the mountains. You feel the erect world of trees and their living vitality while the smell of resin fills you with fresh energy. The air is clear and brisk and has its own peculiar newness as if it was the first air in the world, filled with energy that wakes you up. As you approach the standing trees at the foot of the mountains there is the atmosphere of great forests and silent serenity. Nothing can disturb this place of peaceful power. You are here, and all is exactly as it is supposed to be.

You stand peacefully, drawing in the peace, the pure energy, the inviting light of the stars and the scents of the forest. Then you suddenly discover an opening between the trees and you realize that you are in front of a cave-like opening into the mountain. Everything is calm and quiet and you feel drawn to go inside. As you go in through the opening, you immediately feel you have entered the domain of the mineral kingdom. The atmosphere of massive rocks is everywhere. Even if it is fresh, it is not cold inside. A pleasant coolness and a dim light makes it possible for you to move forward into the mineral world. You move through a passage and suddenly the space opens and you are in a large cavern. You now sense a growing peace within you and you notice the gentle temperature in the cavern. In the dim light, you discover a figure at the other end. You are surprised, but also aware of a subtle friendliness and it seems certain that you are welcome and expected. The figure is not in clear light, but you slightly sense outlines of a face and you get the feeling that this is your companion in the cavern, waiting especially for you.

For a moment, it is as if the walls in the cavern and the mountain itself becomes transparent enough for you to see through it and out into the world. You are shown the portals in the East, South and West. Out there, they are connected with the mountains, forests and cavern here in North. Silently and without words, it is as if you are guided to these directions and made aware that the portals constitute a larger whole. Then your companion in the cavern starts communicating with you. You are not certain whether you simply hear the words inside your head, or if you actually hear them audibly. It really doesn't matter. You are completely focused on the friendly voice that bids you welcome and ask you the question:

*"**What is a portal?** This is an important question. The Sidhe-wisdom can help you. We have learned to be portals, so for us it is natural. For you it implies a new learning and getting used to new things. A portal is an opening making passage and movement possible between one place and another. However, it is also something in itself. It is a relaxed awareness in the open stream. That, which is effortlessly aware, is unwavering in its own way. It is a natural and living force enabling contact. It is a being at peace, letting energy flow. You can only enter a portal because you are a portal yourself. The wisdom of the portal is without beginning and end – everything becomes possible. You are the living portal of your*

life, and when you evolve your capacity to navigate in stillness and movement, in the calm and the flow, new worlds open. A portal is an in-between. A combing conduit. The portal is between-ness. When you breathe it flows up and down in you, and at the same time, you are quietly immobile, resting. It flows in your whole body and around you. What seems separate is connected in the flow. That, which is 'just-next-to', is linked via the portal. You see this magic unfold in the transitions of dusk and dawn, in shadow and shelter, bordering 'in' and 'out'. Where does something begin, and where does it end? You are always on the edge between worlds, but if you do not know it and understand how to navigate, you are stuck in one place only."

The voice stops and in the silence that follows, you slowly become aware that here and there in the rocky walls it sparkles. Shining minerals glitter in the dimly lit cavern. You sense that each and every one of these gleaming stones tells stories and open doors in consciousness if they are touched. You also discover openings to other corridors and remote places. The cavern is a place you can return to repeatedly. Right now your attention is directed towards a faintly illuminated, circular opening between the both of you on the cavern floor. As you look at it you are struck by the gentle, inviting atmosphere and the mild light from below – deep in the underground. Your silent Sidhe-companion approaches you and you get so close that you can see it is an illuminated well leading far down below.

Even though it defies all logic you step out in the light from below and ever so lightly you descend down into the friendly light of the well. You sink and sink, gently and smoothly you surround yourself with the rounded rocks and the blurred light of the well. While you descend, gradually the light grows until you suddenly emerge and land in an open, lighted landscape and stand in the grass, surrounded by living nature, buzzing with life.

Right ahead of you, not far away, you see a standing stone, powerful and with elegant beauty. It is alluring and you get the feeling that the surrounding landscape is connected with it. Slowly and naturally you approach it and sense its silent power. You see delicate, old ornaments on its surface. It radiates with primeval presence and here and there it is partly covered with moss and lichens. You touch it and it feels warm and alive. Immediately as you contact it physically, it is as if many places around in the big landscape light up. You know from within that all these places are outposts of the stone and the connections light up as a delicate, etheric web.

As you remove your hand from the stone, the connected points of light disappear, but immediately when you touch it again, it repeats itself and the lighted web with the points of light reemerge. You realize that the standing stone and your contact with it, is an invitation to you to move out into the landscape around you to discover and find the points of light and what they hide. You lean against the stone with your back, feel its gentle power and look out into the great landscape, and while you feel its living presence it is as if you clearly hear a voice within you saying:

"Welcome to the stone in the North. Look around and connect with nature. See how the landscape is teeming with lighted points connected with the stone where you are now. These lighted points are wild essences. In order to find them you have to leave the stone and then you can't see them. Take your time. Explore and find the essences that can help you on your further journey. They are like magical jewels, full of wisdom. When you hold them gently in your hand and listen to them, they will tell you what they contain, and unfold their story. Make no haste. You can always return to this place and find more. When you are ready, explore on your own and gather your first wild essences. Sense them, look into them and listen to them. May your path be lighted".

For a while you stand in silence and absorb the helping words, while you quietly prepare to walk out into the wondrous landscape in the North, deep under the mountains, the starry heaven and the majestic greatness of the forests. You then let go, leave the friendly stone and walk out into the green world.

What happens out there is entirely your story and what you find are your wild essences. Take care of them and let them guide you. I cannot open them for you, but here I will share a handful of wild essences that I treasure and keep learning from in my own life. I found them during my visit, and they can be expressed in short aphorisms:

Get lost and find your way

It is certain that nothing is certain

The openings are often inches away from where you look

Up is down, out is in – and the opposite

Straight ways are winding, and the shortest is the circle

Follow inspiration no matter where it leads you

The most worn out boots can be your most precious wings.

The Portal of the East

I WILL SING IN THE WIND
CARRESSING THE CHEEK
A HYMN FOR LIFE

A PSALM OF GROWTH
THAT CAN NEVER FADE
ONLY GREENER BECOME

THE DAY BEGINS
IN PEACEFUL BALANCE
FOR LIFE, THE BEAUTIFUL

FROM THE EAST COMES LIGHT
SWEET AS A FEATHER
TO THE GREEN, GREEN GRASS

Qualities: Regeneration, Connectivity, Livingness
Element: Air
Treasure: Sword
Keyword: Life

The blackbird sends its melodic tunes out into the great, open space and you sense a silent inner harmony as you gaze from North towards the East to find the next portal. You have walked out of the cavern and have the mountains and the great forests behind you as a great field of stillness, supporting you in the next phase ahead. As you look towards the East and devote yourself to listening to the captivating song, you realize that it is not night any longer. Morning has broken and the Eastern light is growing on the fresh sky emerging from the nightly peace. As you take it in, you feel how a sunrise within you is also emergent. You turn your attention to your heart-area and sense the delicate rays increase. With the same ease as the small pauses between the ever-changing twitter of birds, you realize that in a blink of an eye you have changed position and are now in the East, facing the rising sun.

It is a very early dawn and you look towards the rays bursting from the horizon. Little by little, the light grows in silence. The sky is vast above you and around you, and now you hear how an increasing choir of birds celebrates sunrise in a louder and louder performance. You are in a clearing with scattered broad-leaved trees, young trees with erect stems and fine, elegant branches. The atmosphere is light and soft in this early morning. Some of the trees are birch trees with light green leaves. Others are young beech trees and there are other types of trees, surrounding you with newly unfolded leaves. The air is crisp with delicate scents of morning dew, spring flowers and fresh earth. Clarity grows and the sky is high. The world is young, new and with an almost audible, crunching readiness to new experiences and adventure.

You enjoy the early morning atmosphere and breathe deeply. In front of you stretch out vast, open fields, filled with grass opening up to the growing light of the daybreak. The green world almost invites you to move towards the sun, but as you stand in the clearing, you quickly discover the gracious figure of a nibbling deer ahead of you. Its elegant body moves silently while it eats grass and occasionally looks around to be sure it is safe. In the silent now, you cautiously follow the watchful movements of the beautiful and shy creature. Suddenly the deer looks towards you and hold its focus right on you. Time seems to be frozen. There is only the deer and you. You look at it. It looks at you. All is gathered in this now. As you forget everything around you, the sunlight increases behind the creature and you are blinded so you can scarcely see it. However, deep within you there is the knowledge that you must follow the deer and walk against the light.

The light intensifies in the East and the glory of the sun crowns the horizon. You cannot see the deer anymore, but you start walking in its direction, moving through the cool grass and noticing how big the space is as you get out of the clearing. A gentle and fresh morning wind waves through the open scenery and plays with the grass. You are one with the widespread fields, the great sky and the living wind as you move forward towards the growing sunrise. Ahead, on the wide plains, you see a grove of trees and bushes, all clad in festive green. There – in the middle of the vast grass-field – it looks like a light green oasis surrounded by deeper green. You are heading towards it, feeling the silent, gentle invitation in your heart, and the vital atmosphere. As you approach, it is as if the grove becomes much bigger and appears as an entire world in itself. When you stand in front of it, you are facing a vibrantly vital, breathing power, as if the grove was a living, green being in itself.

You simply have to stop. It is as a magical world only to be experienced to the full if you are allowed to go there and receive permission. Right in front of you are bushes and smaller trees, filled with a sea of light green leaves in many nuances. It all vibrates with life in a completely new way. It is alive. The grove is a being and the bushes and trees are part of its body. A new, yet strangely familiar sensation is in and around you, beyond explanation, as memories from a distant past, returning in this now. Exactly in this moment, bushes and trees start moving slowly and bend a little to both sides, so you can see a narrow track inside. Very quietly and with great care, almost in slow motion, you move forward in answer to the silent invitation and let yourself be absorbed by the green, leafy world.

Immediately it is as if nothing other than leaves exist. An endless world of leaves in light green nuances. Leaves all around you. You cannot see anything else but leaves. You sense their tender surfaces on your skin while you move forward. As you glide onward it is as if the leaves become alive, also within you, and sometimes they form faces – humanoid and animal-like – and yet not quite as you are accustomed to recognizing it. It is as if the green world enters you and awake something ancient, something pristine. The greenness comes into you and you see endless forests, vast fields of greenness – somehow within you already. Distant, remote worlds, now suddenly within reach. In the center of this extraordinary and yet completely natural world of greenness it is as if all the faces slowly converge into one single face, seeming to be human and yet with the character of the deer all-pervading it. A deer-human? A human deer? It is a face in the middle of greenness with dimly glowing antlers as if the humanoid deer is crowned with a kind of horned glory, surrounded by leaves – bathed in a soft, almost golden light. Before you know it, you hear, as if the living voice of greenness speaks to you:

*"**What is livingness?** What is it to be alive in a new way, from within? Not just to survive, but to be alive in your whole being, mind, psyche and body? We, your Sidhe-relatives, invite you to investigate it and urge you to let go of feeling encapsulated behind your skin. Everything breathes. Everything pulsates. Borders are only superficial. Follow the life-giving trail in everything. Be open to all that offers and infuses life. In reality, you are just as connected to all around you as the branches of a tree, stretching out in many directions with leaflets and leaves.*

In the same way, a delta is life-giver in countless streams, spreading like a fan or like roots or tree-crowns. Life reaches out everywhere, blends, and brings forth renewal. You are streaming and mutable like the clouds in the sky, endlessly changing their forms and blending with each other in new formations and shapes. You are as energetic and crunching as flames, spreading out, dancing and morphing while they warm and reshape substance. Learn from the trees, the rivers, the clouds and the fire. In the connected streams everything is renewed, energies flow and feed living forces. Your inner connectedness is stronger than your ostensible limitation. However, you must let go of your 'business-as-usual-intellect' to wake up to your living connectedness. The mind has a sharpness that is very useful as a tool, but do not identity with it and reduce yourself to the tool – use it wisely as an instrument, serving you and helping you forward. You must let go of deeply carved habits, in order to allow the new flow".

You sense the reality of the words all through your body and awareness. You are not limited but alive in organic osmosis with everything else around you. You breathe with all that lives. You are a tuning fork vibrating with all that is around you, and you can start a new journey, exploring what it is to be in tune with others. While you stand and feel this new clarity, the green around you begins to recede. In front of you, an opening appears and in the open space in the midst of the green hangs a lightening, golden sword in the air, full of the dazzling light of the morning sun. It is an almost blinding, both golden and silvery, sword, floating in front of you – an amazing sight, surprising you and leaving you speechless. The green clearing and the sword is all you can see. Then the same voice continues:

"Welcome to the sword in the East. In the living green a treasure is hidden, a priceless help on the path to renewal. When you open yourself to the living streams, you need to navigate. In order to do this you must know your values and choose what helps you on your way. The living web of life shudders by even the slightest movement, and you must know what you want, and what you do not want, if you are to avoid getting lost in the world of eternal growth and youth. The sword gives you the power and ability, but only when you take it in your hand".

You clearly sense that you have access to the sword and are welcomed. Direction and clarity is needed if you are not to get lost in the green world. It is a delicate balance and the sword must be used with great care so the living energy does not turn barren. Greenness with no direction easily becomes deception, being lost in the currents of the present, as driftwood on open sea. The sword with no sense of delicacy and grace in the now simply is idiocy, foolishness, blind control with no sense of situation. Balance is the art.

Silently and with great respect, you approach the sword, and it is as if you move into a glowing field of high frequency, filled with sounds you cannot hear. Maybe the energy is roaring. Maybe it is a silent wall of sound. It is as if all is thunder but you can't hear anything. As your hand slowly grabs the sword, everything around you becomes crisp and clear as if it was carved in sound. In a flash, you realize where you are in relation to South, West and North. It is as if you hear the directions as sounds or as powerful sources of tunes, reaching you here in the greenness and the silver-golden vibration of the sword of high frequency. Right there in the vital domain of the green world, surrounded by bushes, trees and vegetation, you see shining streams, creating the finest and most delicate web of light. In this web, you see knots and points of condensed light. You see the world green all around you, woven in light with tiny suns where many threads converge. Right there you know that these are the wild essences in the East. They can be found, if you move out from here with the spirit of the sword and in harmony with the living greenness.

This part of the journey is entirely your own. All I can do here is to share some of the wild essences I have found myself. Maybe they show the way. Maybe they stir within you the unraveling of your own essences. The portal in the East is always there and gives its visitors repeated access:

Trust your impressions. Do not add, do not subtract

Listen to everything – follow one thing at a time

Life always finds a way

The untamed Self is barefooted

Leave green traces

The Question is the Answer

You have access to everything – when there is attunement.

The Portal of the South

WHEN THE LIGHT STANDS HIGH
OVER THE MEADOWS OF SUMMER
AND ABUNDANCE IS EVERYWHERE

IT RADIATES WITH A GOLDEN GLOW
IN THE DEPTHS OF THE FORESTS
AND HEAVINESS IS IMMERSED WITHIN LIGHT

THE FORCE LANDS IN THE WOMB OF THE MOTHER
AND THE WORLD IS OPEN TO THE SOUTH

THE BELLS ARE RINGING – SPREADING OUT THEIR WINGS
NOW THE CREATIVE, FIERY SOUND IS HEARD

Qualities: Shapeshifting, Light-imagination, Transformation
Element: Fire
Treasure: Spear
Keyword: Light

You didn't even notice it. Before you looked around you, you were far South. Maybe you were carried to the place on magical moveable branches, or clad in a mighty, flying green leaf. Now you are here in an oak forest with plenty of ferns covering the floor of the woodland. You are surprised and need a little time to land. You inhale the rich and scented forest air and sense the fragrance of soil, moss and herbs. The earth is so full and the air is seething with the atmosphere of summer and sensual energy. The old oak trees have extensive trunks and some of them curve as if frozen in a slow dance. Their age gives you a feeling of calm and depth as if you have landed in a pleasant, sensual density. Slowly and quietly, you begin to move towards the forest, becoming more open to the light. Rays of sunlit brightness play between the leaf-clad branches and you are in a world wrapping you with relaxation in body and emotions. While you move softly, you glide into the atmosphere of the forest, as you become part of the quiet world. A mild coolness emanates from the earth beneath you and although it is a summer day, there is a freshness in the air, a living vitality making it easy for you to move between the trees.

Somewhere is a cuckoo with its characteristic sound. You become aware of other birds too, and a red squirrel catches your attention on its way up a branch not far from you. It does not seem frightened and takes its time in small, abrupt movements – almost as if you were not there. While you stand, engulfed by the scenery, you slowly notice a kind of presence from the oak trees gradually stepping forth through the branches around you. You have not expected this and to your quiet amazement, it is humanoid, green figures in some unknown way gradually condensing into visibility. You are not frightened by the unusual sight, but very surprised. Perhaps because of the tranquil atmosphere, infusing you with calmness. On the other hand, you may simply be very open to what may unfold.

The figures have a graceful, feminine look and appear as if clad in the poetry of nature. Their bodies are surrounded with, or even made of, green ivy and they radiate a weak, warm light. They move very silently and radiate a dim, warm light. They proceed with grace and dignity, very beautiful and delicate. It is a strange experience as they radiate something that seems humanlike, and yet you know they definitely do not originate from your world. Their figures seem solid in their own way, but they also appear plastic and full of inner light as if the chosen form can shift at any time if needed. One of them looks at you and again you sense a distinct peacefulness combined with a kind of wildness and sparkling power. These graceful females have a great power, and if the situation dictated it, they could appear frightening if they changed their energetic mode. They are definitely guardians, and you know deep within that their gentle look is coupled with invisible power. They could turn into scary apparitions and probably keep anything unwelcome out of this forest. However, to you, they are silent, welcoming companions approaching you. Suddenly one of them address you with a mild, feminine voice, saying:

"**What is transformation?** We have approached your world so you can sense us. We are very close to you, and yet we seem to be in another reality – or submitting to other rules than you. Now we meet and it is not just a fantasy, it is real. Our meeting can be transformative if we allow it to be so. The question is what we are ready to accept as real. The Sidhe-wisdom says that transformation is the most natural thing in the world as it is the art of change. Nothing is fixed forever. Everything is in constant movement and in this alteration; miraculous transformations are possible when initiated from within. It is not "hocus-pocus" or "humbug" as you occasionally say. It is form-change. It is inner conditions taking outer forms. In order to open for such a reality, preconditioned opinions must be put aside. They will only hinder and create blockage. A playful lightness is needed, together with a smiling openness and the light of joy. Transformation is a journey, a continued process with many layers and aspects. As a beginning, we would like to show you some of this, but you must continue yourself. It is not something that can be given. It is an inner experience that must be acquired and made natural. Transformation is saying yes to birth and death, to the ever becoming of change in form, rising from within. The art of transformation is the most natural and common art. Yet, it is miraculous because it demonstrates reality as amazing, surprising, and full of great challenges and blessings."

The green figures now move very close to you so you can feel their atmosphere very clearly. One of them reaches out and gently touches your brow with a finger. In the very same moment, everything disappears around you. Instead, you can see the whole oak forest completely changed. All around you, the crooked branches turn into troll-like faces with weird grimaces. All kinds of forms you believed to be trees, forest floor and green growth also turn out to be hidden figures able to perform grotesque and quirky movements and make the most bizarre faces and attitudes. Figures all around you become alive. You could not see them before, but now they appear and the forest swarms with hidden life. It is a mixture of graceful and grotesque, awkward, enchanting and strange forms. Some of it appears quite frightening, other figures seem enticing and curious, and yet others again look incredibly beautiful. It is all morphing and in movement. The atmosphere is exuberant and not gloomy. You sense a facet of reality normally ascribed to fantasy novels and science fiction films. Here it is real. It really IS. Perhaps you don't know how to describe it, but it is around you and you cannot deny it. Normal rules and laws for up and down, factual and fictional, real and illusory are blurred in the zone where you are. You are completely awake, not dreaming, and it is happening around you.

In the midst of all, it seems to start glowing ahead of you in the living jumble and you see that the lively brushwood in a clearing near you also has bushes with ripe blackberries and raspberries. Straight through them there is a narrow trail leading forward. Again, you sense that you are invited, and you pluck some of the berries and enjoy their juicy taste while it whirls around you with strange beings – smiling and making grimaces. It is as if you are surrounded by a childish happiness, very contagious and making you smile yourself while you follow the small trail and feel encouraged by the beings around you. The sounds of the birds grow bigger and the forest becomes more open – and you are in the most wonderful world. In the blink of an eye, you become aware that the many creatures around you are not visible any longer. You sense their presence, and the atmosphere of the green, feminine guardians is still there. However, you are back and breathe in the well-known forest.

Here where you are now, you can see a winding track, leading further down and into the Northern entrance of a mighty valley in the South, curved and surrounded by trees at the Northern end. The light and the open space is calling and now you must continue. While walking you start seeing the edge of the forest and it widens to the sides. You continue to wander down into the valley, surrounded by forest along its edges. The light of the sun and the summer meets you in the open air. Insects are busy around the many flowers and the blinding disk of the sun is high in the sky as you walk down into the great, rich valley. As you descend, you discover a grass covered hill, right at the southern end of the valley. On its top stands a single tree. It seems obvious to you to approach this exposed hill with the tree, giving shadow in the noonday sun. You soon find out it is an apple tree and as you walk up the hill, you find it very comfortable to sit under the tree, covered by its gentle crown, and enjoy the view to the South.

Gazing further southward, you see something peculiar. Even further down at the end of the valley there is yet another hill. It seems like you are on a leyline, or at least that the hills are placed deliberately as focalizers of energy. You smile and relax, and you let your back lean on the apple tree, and it is pleasant and cool although it is noon and summer and clear, blue sky. As you sink into the atmosphere of the protective tree, you hear a clear voice:

"Welcome to the spear in the South. In front of you is the hill of the spear, holding the secret of transformation. If hidden resources shall be set free, it is necessary to apply the particular light-imagination that releases the bound treasures. There has to be a decisiveness to set free the imprisoned power and let it manifest. You can only do this by guiding the light with a loving purpose. The spear of light and purpose can only be used when guided by the heart-sun. Behold the spear in front of you!"

Looking towards the hill ahead of you it is as if the noonday rays of the sun concentrate in a vertical flow downwards. They gather and reach down in a blinding intensity as they hit the hill from above. In that blinding moment, they reveal a shining spear, now standing on the hill, exactly on its top. When looking at this stunning view, you become aware that exactly from here there is contact to the portals in the North, East and West. Is seems that because of the revealed spear you are simultaneously present in all four places.

From the spear shines a honey golden light and the radiance explodes silently in a cascade of fireflies, dancing in the air around the spear and the hill. It is a marvelous spectacle. As the almost blinding radiance gradually decreases and leaves the spear on the hill, the many fireflies seek out from it in all directions as they carry a trail in thin, glowing tracks behind them. They spread out in the landscape of the great valley, even up to the trees along the upper edges. Everywhere the fireflies descend and when they land, light flashes brightly for a moment as if they mark the spot. Immediately you know that these are the wild essences shown to you before the fireflies dissipate. All that is left is the valley and your knowledge that the essences are out there in the South, and you have access to them.

Again, I remind you that you must do your own research and discover what is there for you. All I can do is to share with you some of the wild essences I have found here in the South.

Look to the side

Either-Or is never enough

Delight in sensing

Playful mischief is a great teacher

Discover beauty in ugliness

Everything tells a story

The natural is full of wonder

The Portal of the West

WITH SPIRIT WE JOIN
AND OPEN IN THE WEST
A FIERY SYMPHONY OF COLORS

LET THE SOUNDS WAVE
AS LIVING STREAMS
IN THE ALCHEMY OF THE SOUL

AND THE CIRCLE ENDS AT THE EVENING SEA
AND THE FORCES ARE SET FREE

THE HEALING GRAIL WILL RELEASE
THE DEEP MAGIC OF WHOLENESS

Qualities: Weaving, Life-Musicality, Magic
Element: Water
Treasure: Cauldron
Keyword: Healing

You only had to look towards the West, and there you were. With the lightning speed of the spear, you arrived in a vast, hilly landscape, with torn and craggy rocks here and there, mixed with green vegetation and small bushes clad in the many-colored hues of autumn. Now you are here in the midst of it all. The atmosphere is cool and a fresh wind blows over the hills. The most notable thing you experience is the sound of water in a brook close by, moving towards the West. The sound is fresh and twinkling and you feel cleansed by it as you stand here in the afternoon in the windswept open. Far away, you hear seagulls screaming to each other.

The place fills you with energetic vitality and you are clear in the head. You look a little around you and then walk to the brook to look at its graceful, flowing movements over small stones and pebbles. The sounds are attractive and enticing. The sound of water is lively and chattering as it hastens from land to sea. It has an atmosphere of raw purity, inviting you to taste it. You kneel and let your hand wash in the cold stream and then you collect the cold liquid in your palms and quench your thirst. Refreshing, clear fluid with a frail taste of mountains and green vegetation. As you take all this in with delight, a picture flashes in your head and you see a stone cottage, a simple cottage in an open landscape. Even though you don't think you can know it as a fact, yet you still feel the water and the cottage are connected. Maybe it is a sign. You rise and look around you. As it is you cannot see anything specific apart from the wide landscape, but you sense that perhaps the small brook can show you the way, so you decide to follow its way towards the sea.

At a quiet pace, you start walking further to the West, with the wind in your hair and a feeling inside, unexplainable, but still there. After some time the landscape becomes more wild and uneven and you walk on the top of the hills to get a better view. Maybe, after traveling through all the places from North to East, South and now West, you have stopped being amazed about things, or are you just getting used to guidance on your way? Further ahead in a lowered opening, covered with grass, you see the contours of something resembling a man-made building. You speed somewhat up and yes, as you get closer you are sure it is a primitive, little cottage, built of local stones from the landscape. As you approach it, to your surprise – or to your expectation, it's not clear which – you see that the door is open. Can it be more obvious? You must be welcomed. The brook passes nearby. You walk to the entrance and knock on the side of the open wooden-door. Nobody answers and yet you have the feeling that you are allowed to enter. In a friendly tone, you say "Hello!" You duck your head as you look inside. The warmth and the sound of a crackling hearth strike you, although the room inside is not big. You choose to trust your feeling and enter the cottage.

You have scarcely got accustomed to the dim light inside; before you realize you are not alone in the cottage. In a chair to your right, opposite the hearth, a woman sits. She silently bows her head and bids you welcome, pointing at a chair close to the hearth. Quietly you take your seat. The warmth from the hearth and the smell of burning logs makes you relaxed and you smile at the woman. She is dressed in green and brown colors and has a gentle, friendly face, surrounded by big hair, looking slightly wild, but not in a primitive way. She seems very human and at the same time, it is as if her features carry all the features of nature itself, brought here, inside the cottage. It may sound odd, and perhaps it is. It is as if the depth of the mountains in the North, the waving grass in the East and the fragrant flowers in the South are with her right here, in the cottage in the West. Her look and face seems to capture the essence of all of it, and while you are lost in all this, she breaks the silence:

*"**What is magic?** You have traveled to the stone in North, the sword in East and the spear in South. Now the circle is completed here in the West. It is a magical journey, an opening to your Sidhe-nature enabling you to become more human. But what is the nature of magic? It is something entirely different from so-called "magic" as you normally use the word. It is several things and has deeper meanings. Basically, the soul of magic is the green heart of being natural. It is how life is. We could also say that magic is more subtle energies penetrating and uplifting more dense and heavy energies. Seen from the outside it may look supernatural, but this is how nature functions. We could also say that magic is when the supernatural becomes ordinary because we accept that reality is far greater than we assumed. The art of magic is the very essence and green heart of the noble art of living. The Sidhe-wisdom shows us that deep magic takes place when we contact the living flow of wholeness. It is like music opening the closed rooms and making the soul dance with its creation. The inner and outer sing and move in living attunement. It is a dance transforming through its rhythm,*

its melodies and its deep harmony. You are invited if you have awakened to the musical longing of your heart."

Before you even get time to reflect on her words, you see that she has a harp standing in the shadow beside her. She leans against it and starts playing. The delicate, tantalizing sounds fill the room of the cottage and you lean back in your comfortable chair and go with it. With your inner vision, you see how music lives in the murmuring and chatting of the brooks, bending and curving towards the great sea in the West. You hear melodies in the wind, shaking in bushes and trees. To the North, East, and South for the first time you hear the portals as living music, each with their clear characteristics. The four gateways turn into a symphonic harmony, connecting with the earth and all living beings.

As you sense the sound of the stone in the North, the sword in the East and the spear in the South, your consciousness is drawn down beneath the cottage in a bubbling tide, deep below in the underground. Down here, in the rocky depth, in a huge grotto or mighty cave you see a gigantic, bowl-shaped rock, constantly overflowing with living streams of water rushing to all sides in a never-ending movement. Through pores, cracks, and openings in the rocks the water is led further out and up towards the surface of the earth, dripping forth as fountains and springs then becoming small streams, brooks and rivers, all heading toward the sea.

Beholding the captivating sight, you know that the bowl of rock is the cauldron, the fourth treasure or hallow in the West, just as you know that the water of life overflowing from it, is bathed in the light from the heart of the earth and the dazzling streams of the stars. In the music, you hear the voice of the woman, once again:

"Welcome to the cauldron in the West. When you drink from the fountains leading towards the sea, you know that you drink the water of life from this hallowed treasure, and you will be renewed from within so you can see and sing and move to the dances of the living life. The healing power of the water will

nourish you and strengthen your growth as the new human being that has become the living stone. Go out, drink, and meet the world. A new dance can begin".

In an instant, you open your eyes and you are back at the hearth in the stone cottage. In front of you, the chair is empty and the harp is gone. The hearth still glows with orange embers, it is warm and you rise, filled with gratitude to the wise harpist, still with echoes of the music as a silent dance within you. You go outside in the fresh air and close the cottage door behind you, as you decide to follow the brook to the sea. Occasionally you stop, kneel and collect water. Some of it you drink, and the rest you wash yourself with, feeling fresher and more awake than ever. You notice how the water dances around the stones and glides round their hard surfaces. After some time you reach the great sea to the West, seemingly stretching endlessly. The sun is setting and a light stratus creates the most beautiful soft and red poetry on the sky, as you walk along the beach. Nobody needs to tell you. Right here among the pebbles, the seaweed and all that is carried up here from the sea, you will find your wild essences in the West. Here they are. You will never run out of supply and you can always return.

The only thing I can do here is to share some of the wild essences I have collected myself in the West, which I gladly share with you.

When you smile and laugh with lightness you inhale Starlight

Listen to the Inner Sounds

Create Lyrical Attunement

Root yourself and drink Nectar

Discover Deep Magic

Follow the Call of the Wild, Green Heart

You are the Dancing Stone

Open Landscape

The cycle is completed. All four portals have been encountered, and shared some of their wisdom. We are now in open landscape and the wild alliance can gestate within us.

There is a deep, etymological connection between incarnation and land, and it is worth sharing. To incarnate in the fullest sense is 'to land' and fully embody the organic form-life with all the inner life. The meaning of the word 'land' – as in landscape – really is 'to land', to descend and embody. The land is the Mother, the divine feminine taking form. She is the landscape, every landscape, be it small or big, inner or outer. The land is 'that which lands'. When we incarnate we 'land in the land'. To land literally means to arrive, to get into contact, to be rooted. When we arrive in the land, we can also land in ourselves. We can stand on the ground and root. Then we can become the portals we are destined to be. The Mother is living matter taking form as the landscape. We become the true indigenous people when we are born into the Motherland, into the landscape. We all need to land and become indigenous inhabitants of the Motherland. From here the journey can start. All scenery can become part of the Motherland if we really 'land' there and embrace the place. Perhaps it is a landscape. It can also be a cityscape or a seascape, or it can be a soundscape or a dreamscape. Any possible scenery of forms – inner or outer – is part of the great Motherland, the nurturing Mother.

Fjeldur has shared a Sidhe perspective about space as landscape, and it seems relevant to pass it on here, after we have completed the landscape journey to the four hallows. Every space is a living landscape. Can we bring this attunement into our lives? Landscapes have nodes or energy knots, centering points of component parts with specific roles and capacities. They can also be seen as musical notes. In their interplay they are parts of the music being performed as the landscape itself. Perceived from within, a landscape is music being played perpetually as a living symphony or piece of music within a greater music. This landscape world is life perceived from within.

It has been called the *'inscape'* – the inner landscape – and it relates both to yourself as landscape and to the greater surroundings you are part of.

The landscape has its own rhythm, pulse or timing. It is mostly connected with the underground or the depth, at one with the inner light of Gaia. Connecting with your own underground gives you a sense of your rhythm. Attune with the deep below, within you and within any landscape. What is felt, what is heard, what is seen? The landscape has its peculiar melodies or melodical themes. They are mainly distributed on the surface and constitute its content or mass. Living creatures are the nodes or knots in these melodies. Attune with your conscious world and connect with your signature tunes. Which themes resonate within you? What do they connect with? What stories do they tell? The landscape attempts to create a specific harmony of its own. This concordance is mainly perceived in the upper part of the landscape, in the aerospace, as a crowning feature, but it permeates the totality as well. What is the nature of the harmony within you, attempting to manifest? What is its message? What is its nature?

As you walk in nature, you are hiking in the living landscape of Gaia. It is the same as your own Gaian nature within, your subpersonalities in the subconscious, your voices and talents as well as your wider possibilities and visions. It reflects beautifully in your body with its regions, limbs, organs and orchestrated totality. Your inner Sidhe is your landscape artist. It is your inherited, natural landscaper, always focused on the totality or wholeness. Sometimes you need to inspect how it is going with the creatures within you. Are they well and thriving? Do they need something? At other times, you connect with the rhythm and deeper parts. Are they okay? Is the grounding healthy and attuned with the rest? Do you need to recalibrate or connect with other rhythms?

Regenerating Connectivity

Leaving the self-limited flatland of surface-mentality, and reconnecting with the deep landscape of life, is a great liberation. It is an entrance to clear air, sparkling water, bright light and rich soil. In this expansive, huge and ever growing continent of unfolding life, there is a freshness and a vitality that cannot be compared with anything superficial. Everything in and around you is alive and connecting with everything else.

Being in the deep landscapes of life, and the connectivity between all living entities, opens you to great regeneration. From the deep ground of the land, the depth of Gaia, emerges a continues flow of rejuvenating forces and energies. They add to the quickening and restorative processes of your body and psyche. It is a subtle, organic flow, supporting all life processes and stimulating your continued awakening. It also connects with your sensual intelligence, the healthy and immediate understanding of vitality, and of how you need to affirm and connect with wholeness, repeatedly. You are always in wholeness. You are embedded in the landscape of life, in the world of the great Mother. From her nurturing richness comes restorative and sensual vitality. She gives you prosperity through her etheric vivacity.

Behind and through the outer forms is a continuum of juicy, fructifying movement. When we connect with it with no reservation, this all-pervasive tide brings pure enjoyment, pure delight. Its sensual presence imbues us and we are immediately connected with the energies of organic meshwork everywhere in nature. It has so many hues, fragrances, tunes and nuances, yet in itself, it is not divided. It is an awakening to refined simplicity, imbuing and impregnating with the juicy nectar of delight and inspiration. It is the very nature of joyful delight, full of innocence and fresh energy, inspiring you to renewal. Open yourself to this world of regenerating delight. Perceive it with all your senses. Open yourself to the peripheral wisdom and invite it into your center.

An aspect of this is attunement to sounds. Your inner Sidhe is a vibratory system, acutely sensitive towards other systems, like a hybrid of a hummingbird and a butterfly, and yet grounded with the anchoring of humaneness. When you establish yourself as a vibratory portal, open to any landscape – outer as well as inner – you can be a bridge. You can learn 'in-between-ness' and become aware of the world of portals. There is a wisdom in guarding the thresholds. There is a wisdom in hospitality across the thresholds, between worlds. In addition, there is a wisdom in being an agent of regeneration and renewal across borders. The world needs this healing, restoring function.

There is a treasure house in discovering and activating what have been called signatures. Reading, integrating and working with living signatures is an ancient Sidhe art. A signature is a pattern of wholeness manifesting spontaneously in living, meaningful configurations. In the human world, we partly know it as 'meaningful coincidences' or synchronicity. It may manifest in meeting somebody or something at a very specific place, with astonishing timing and with great meaning. All involved elements are like syllables in a word or sentence uttered in that situation. We meet the right person at the right place in the right time – and things open up. We receive a thing in the very moment we ask for guidance, and it helps us to understand what is needed. We miss a bus and go to a place we would not have thought about, and it turns out the place is what we sought. The wonderful examples are endless, and they are like starting a new conversation with life about the art of living.

In the Sidhe context, it is always in some way related to nature, and the meaningful coincidences are 'signatures' with a specific color, quality, tune or meaning. Walking or being in nature is an opportunity to link up with the great healer, or the connective agent. There is a teaching in opening up to living signatures in nature, inviting them to help us reconnect with the meaningful flow. It is like configurations making deep sense. We cannot always understand the full significance when it happens, but it is like several words or elements coming together in a statement. Alternatively, it can be like spontaneous music, manifesting in a coherence or situational harmony. It makes sense and you get the message. It may be difficult to explain logically, but there is an inner knowing and a feeling of 'this-is-right' – sometimes called intuition. If followed, it will turn out to be right. You may struggle to uncover it, but it is deeply meaningful when it finally appears. This is part of the deep magic when your inner Sidhe awakes. Wholeness speaks to us and we can uncover the message and integrate it into our life.

Imagining into the Light

We have imagined ourselves into the confined smallness of superficial life. Light-filled imagination will help us open the doors again into the larger life of beauty and greatness of heart. This noble art is an ancient Sidhe-craft, and it can become a great helper on your way through the maze of human crises and challenges.

Sometimes you need to apply the *'sprinkler approach'*. As a gardener your inner Sidhe needs to spray a mizzle of joy, like descending vapor, or drizzle a fine, misty rain of energy into something. This dispersing is like the role of a spiritual nebulizer spraying living light into all affected parts, thereby helping them to reconnect with wholeness. Being in a situation with difficulties you can use your light-filled imagination and sprinkle light from different angles as you move. Where is the undiscovered opportunity? Where does the potential hide? Gently spray optimism and faith into the corners and on stairways into places yet to be discovered. Envisioning the hidden potential and insisting on fostering growth is a great helper in many life situations.

At other times, you need to apply the *'dragon approach'*, intervening with your creative imagination and building forms from within. Here your Sidhe-landscaper can rearrange, move, dig and mold. It is performed with your light-imagination always looking for the shining heart in a given part, inviting the brightness to surface and shine. You help it to manifest by your attuned, assisting imagination. This can only be done if you don't have a predetermined plan. You have to give in to the process, focused on wholeness and with a spontaneous intention, relying on the situation and the help you always receive from greater wholeness when you are open to it.

You can then activate your natural, creative imagination, trusting what you sense with a gentle attitude. It cannot be forced or imposed. It cannot be planned. It is not-planned planning. You need to 'get lost' in order to find guidance. Imagination must be on free ground, in open landscape, to find the best ways and to weave patterns of connective energy. Using the light-filled imagination and riding on the gentle waves, you become the Dragon Rider – or the Serpent Rider. You are not afraid to enter dark places because you know that there is a hidden light in the heart of it.

With your inner Sidhe nature, you can encounter so-called ugliness, twisted energies and heavy conditions. You will experience the amazing shapeshifting of the landscapes of the mind and psyche and see how seemingly dense heaviness turns into promising gestalts when met with the gentle light of appreciative imagination. As the Dragon Rider, you trust the transformative power. Attuned with the waving currents you ride with the inventive winds of the moment, always focused upon openings and helping wholeness to manifest. It is a noble Sidhe art; one you can unfold in your own life.

Magical Weaver

Your inner Sidhe is your weaver, creating the crochet with living fabric or knitting patterns in breathing flow. Sidhe-wisdom is multi-tasking organically in light. It is sensing wholeness from within and weaving the strands of light that connect, heal and promote wholeness. It is an ancient art, originating partly from the stars and from the earth itself. It is possible because of the inner, organic connectedness that is so natural and effortless for the inner Sidhe.

Ultimately, the wisdom of the portals, the landscaping, the light-imagination and the weaving in wholeness, is the awakening of life-musicality, the creative tonality becoming an integrated part of all of you. This is *the Living Stone* - or *the Living Dancer* – grounded and moving. You become the Lyrical Attuner, the Magical Weaver.

You are the Magical Weaver
Take on your Mantle of Nobleness
Erect and awake you stand
Guarding the Thresholds

You are the Magical Weaver
Attune your Heart with Joy
Open your Living Cauldron
Sharing the Spirit of Love

You are the Magical Weaver
Move as the Living Dancer
Gracefully bridging the Chasm
Releasing New Life into the World

COMING HOME
AS THE STAR-GAIAN HUMAN

Is this simply too far out, like a fairy tale that is simply 'not for real'? You be the judge. If you can hear tunes of a new music, together with protesting voices, then do not forget to listen to the protesters. What do they really say? Are they children of the cynical mentality, needing a lot of love and space to heal? Are they concerned if we become too unrealistic, but deep down they really want to sing and dance? What about the music itself? Do you have to reject it because of present conflicts? Can you abandon the heart of it all and sell yourself to the highest bidder? Not without losing the very essence of who you are. Therefore, let us affirm a resounding YES to the music, amidst the chaos and cacophony. We are in a turbulent world. Exactly because of this, we must insist on the wings of innocence and the feet of the dancer – bringing it forth in our human lives.

We are coming home again, returning to the Hobbit House. Yet, it is an entirely new beginning. We reenter our home, embracing the depth, embracing the height – in the present here and now. This is our new role as co-creative, universal beings with a conscious, personal self. We learn to listen to wholeness and sing the songs of winged grounding. At first in bits and pieces. Later we learn to bring it together in greater sweeps.

As the new Indigenous Star-Gaian Humans, we are creating the song-lines never heard before. We follow the vision track, combining the Stars above and the Earth below with the Land we are in – to become co-creators of living wholeness. Our human characteristic is the burning heart, compassionate and like a warm fire, full of hospitality and kindness. Combined with the sense of purpose we have extracted from the strife and turmoil, we offer the flaming heart of compassion. Bringing forth our inner Sidhe, we let the lyrical merge with the logical. As musicians, singers and dancers we bring life to the standing stones. Calling forth our inner Angel, we let universal inviolability and joyful innocence merge with the personal life. The result is a work in progress, expressing itself in endless variations and stages. We can rest assured that we are the new form of Gaian Pilgrims, embodying the synthesis as Angelic-Sidhe-Humans. We could call it the emerging Star-Gaian Human, embodying Sky and Earth through the Fiery Heart.

WILD ALLIANCE MANDALA

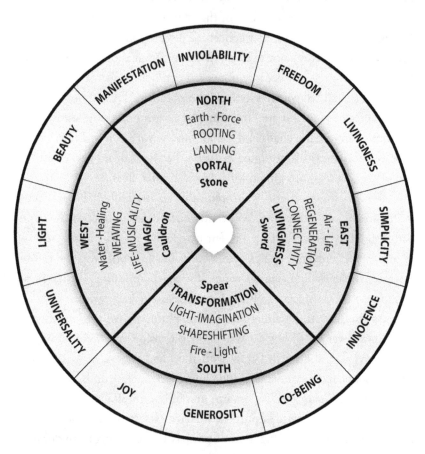

LITERATURE

SELECTED BOOKS ABOUT ANGELS & NATURE SPIRITS

A compilation: *Devas and Men*, The Theosophical Publishing House 1977, ISBN: 0-8356-7518-2.

Alice A. Bailey: *A Treatise on Cosmic Fire*, Lucis Press LTD, Tenth Printing 1973.

William Bloom: *Working with Angels, Fairies and Nature Spirits*, Judy Piatkus (Publishers) 1998, ISBN: 0-7499-1904-3.

Peter Dawkins: Zoence - *An Introduction to the Basic Principles and Practices of Zoence*, Wigmore Publications 1995, ISBN: 0-946982-08-2.

Peter Dawkins: Zoence – *the Science of Life*, Samuel Weiser 1998, ISBN: 1-57863-042-8.

Dora van Gelder: *The Real World of Fairies*, The Theosophical Publishing House 1977, ISBN: 0-8356-0497-7.

Geoffrey Hodson: *Fairies at Work and at Play*, The Theosophical Publishing House 1982, ISBN: 0-8356-0553-1.

Geoffrey Hodson: *The Kingdom of Faerie*, The Theosophical Publishing House 1927, repr. 1993, The Banton Press, ISBN: 1 85652 136 2.

Geoffrey Hodson: *The Brotherhood of Angels and of Men*, The Theosophical Publishing House 1928, repr. 1982, ISBN: 0-8356-0559-0.

Geoffrey Hodson: *The Angelic Hosts*, Kessinger Pub Co. 2003, ISBN-13: 978-0766158085

Geoffrey Hodson: *Man, the Triune God*, Publ. 1932, Kessinger Pub Co, ISBN-13: 978-0766102408

Geoffrey Hodson: *Be Ye Perfect*, The Theosophical Publishing House 1928.

Geoffrey Hodson: *The Supreme Splendour*, The Theosophical Publishing House, repr. 1986, ISBN: 0-8356-9296-4.

Geoffrey Hodson: *The Coming of the Angels*, Rider & Co., 1932, repr., The Banton Press 1993, ISBN: 1-85652-137-0.

Geoffrey Hodson: *The Kingdom of the Gods*, The Theosophical Publishing House 1952, repr. 1987, ISBN: 81-7059-060-1.

Geoffrey Hodson: *Clairvoyant Investigations*, The Theosophical Publishing House 1984, ISBN: 0-8356-0585-X.

Geoffrey Hodson: *Light of the Sanctuary*, The Theosophical Publishers, Inc. 1988, ISBN: 971-91132-0-0.

Dorothy MacLean: *To Hear the Angels Sing*, Lorian Press 2008, ISBN: 978-0-936878-01-0.

Dorothy MacLean: *Call of the Trees*, Lorian Press 2006, ISBN: 0-936878-13-4

Dorothy MacLean: *Seeds of Inspiration*, The Lorian Association 2004, ISBN: 0-936878-08-8.

David Spangler: *Techno-Elementals*, LorianPress 2012, ISBN 13: 978-0-936878-59-1

The Findhorn Community: *The Findhorn Garden*, Perennial (HarperCollins) 1976, ISBN-13: 978-0060905200

SELECTED BOOKS ABOUT THE SIDHE & FAERIE

AE (George William Russell): *The Candle of Vision*, Quest Books 1974, ISBN: 0-8356-0445-4.

AE (G. W. Russell): *The Descent of the Gods, part 3*, ed. By Raghaven & Nandini Iyer, Colin Smythe 1988, ISBN: 0-901072-44-3.

Jeremy Berg: *Faerie Blood*, Lorian Press 2013, ISBN: 10: 0-936878-63-0.

Jeremy Berg: *A Knight to Remember*, Lorian Press 2015, ISBN: 978-0-936878-71-3.

W. Y. Evans-Wentz: *The Fairy-Faith in Celtic Countries*, Dover Publications 2002, ISBN 0-486-42522-3.

Orion Foxwood: *The Faery Teachings*, R. J. Stewart Books 2007, ISBN: 978-0-9791402-2-8.

Brian & Wendy Froud: *Faeries Tales*, ABRAMS 2014, ISBN: 978-1-4197-1386-6.

Brian Froud: *Good Faeries – Bad Faeries*, Simon & Schuster Editions 1998, ISBN: 0-684-84781-7.

Brian Froud: *Brian Froud's World of Faerie,* IMAGINOSIS, Insight Editions 2007, ISBN: 978-1-933784-13-7.

Brian & Wendy Froud: *The Heart of Faerie Oracle*, ABRAMS 2010, ISBN: 978-

0-8109-8823-1.

Brian Froud & John Matthews: *How to see Faeries*, ABRAMS 2011, ISBN: 978-0-9109-9750-9.

Diarmuid Mac Manus: *Irish Earth Folk*, The Devin-Adair Company 1959, Library of Congress 59-13563.

John Matthews: *The Sidhe – Wisdom from the Celtic Underworld*, Lorian Press 2007, ISBN 0-936878-05-3.

John Matthews: *Celtic Myths & Legends*, PITKIN GUIDES, ISBN: 978-1-84165-054-8.

John Michell: *The Earth Spirit – Its Ways, Shrines and Mysteries*, Thames and Hudson 1975, ISBN: 0-500-81011-7.

David Spangler: *Subtle Worlds: An Explorer's Field Notes*, Lorian Press 2010, ISBN: 10: 0-936878-26-6.

David Spangler, art by Jeremy Berg: *Card Deck of the Sidhe*, Lorian Press 2011, ISBN: 978-0-936878-36-2.

David Spangler: *A Midsummers Journey with the Sidhe*, Lorian Press 2011, ISBN: 978-0-936878-52-2.

David Spangler: *Starheart and other stories*, Lorian Press 2013, ISBN 10: 0-936878-65-7.

David Spangler: *Partnering with Earth – The Incarnation of a Soul*, Lorian Press 2013, ISBN 13: 978-0-936878-60-7.

David Spangler: *Conversations with the Sidhe*, Lorian Press 2014, ISBN: 978-0-936878-67-6.

R. J. Stewart: *Earth Light*, Mercury Publishing 1998, ISBN: 1-892137-01-1.

R. J. Stewart: *Power Within the Land*, Mercury Publishing 1998, ISBN: 1-892137-00-3.

R. J. Stewart: *The well of Light*, R. J. Stewart Books 2006, ISBN: 978-0-9791402-1-1.

R. J. Stewart: *The Living World of Faery*, Mercury Publishing 1999, ISBN: 1-892137-09-7.

RECOMMENDED WEBSITES

Lorian Association: www.lorian.org
David Spangler: www.lorianassociation.com
Lorian Press: www.lorianpress.com
R. J. Stewart: www.rjstewart.org
Ian Rees: www.annwnfoundation.com
John Matthews: www.hallowquest.org.uk
Deborah Koff-Chapin: www.touchdrawing.com
Orion Foxwood: www.orionfoxwood.com
Brian Froud: www.worldoffroud.com
Peter Dawkins: www.peterdawkins.com

Søren Hauge (born 1961) is a Danish spiritual teacher, counselor and author. He lives in the southern part of the city of Aarhus on mainland Jutland, Denmark. He has been married to his wife Jette since 1987 and they are parents to two adult daughters, Helene and Johanne. Søren has been a spiritual teacher since 1981 and for three decades he was a leader, teacher and organizer within the Theosophical movement in Scandinavia. He has an MA in History of Ideas and Philosophy from Aarhus University and is the author of fourteen books in Danish, *The Wild Alliance* being his first in the English language. Together with Kenneth Sørensen he has developed a new Energy Psychology with a special focus on educating people in Energy Typology and the SoulFlow Method. Søren is a Lorian Associate, and he has been working with Incarnational Spirituality since 2007. Since 2009, he has also had a private practice as a counselor, specializing in helping people with SoulFlow, Energy Psychology and spiritual counseling.

You can find him at www.sorenhauge.com & www.soulflow.nu

CPSIA information can be obtained
at www.ICGtesting.com
Printed in the USA
BVHW031244080422
633577BV00005B/1354